DR. JOSEPH MURPHY

MAGIC OF FAITH

SANAGE
PUBLISHING HOUSE

Paperback: 978-819592497-4

Any references to historical events, real people, or real places are used fictitiously. Names, characters, and places are products of the author's imagination.

Printed by:

Sanage Publishing House LLP
Mumbai, India

sanagepublishing@gmail.com

Dr. Joseph Denis Murphy (May 20, 1898 – December 16, 1981) was an Irish-born American author and New Thought minister, ordained in Divine Science and Religious Science. Dr. Joseph Murphy has been acclaimed as a major figure in the human potential movement, the spiritual heir to writers like James Allen, Dale Carnegie, Napoleon Hill, and Norman Vincent Peale and a precursor and inspirer of contemporary motivational writers and speakers.

He was one of the Best-selling authors in the mid-twentieth century. His book "The PowerOf Your Sub-Conscious Mind" has sold millions of copies and has been translated into thirty languages. This book has never been out of print and is still one of the best sellers in the self-help genre.

CONTENTS

THE SONG OF TRIUMPH

"*Tell me, O thou whom my soul loveth, where thou feedest, where thou makest THY FLOCK to rest at noon?*"

"*Behold, thou ART fair, my love; behold, thou ART fair; thou HAST doves' eyes.*"

"*He brought me to the banqueting house, and his banner over me WAS love.*" "*His left hand IS under my head, and his right hand doth embrace me.*"

"*My beloved spake, and said unto me, Rise up, my love, my fair one, and come away.*

"*For lo, the winter is past, the rain is over AND gone;*

"*The flowers appear on the earth; the time of the singing of BIRDS is come, and the voice of the turtle is heard in our land;*

"*Arise, my love, my fair one, and come away.*

"*My beloved IS mine, and I AM his: he feedeth among the lilies.*

It is inconceivable that any anthology could be written wherein *The Song of Solomon* would not be included. It is really one of the most inspired parts of the Bible. *The Song of Solomon* reveals God as the Great Lover. It is ecstatic and thrilling.

In order to lead the triumphant life, you must be moved by Love. You can go wild in the joy of being actually drunk with the Spirit. In other words by singing the Song of God, you become God-intoxicated and fired with Divine enthusiasm, thereby expressing more and more of Divine love and joy every day.

You sing the Song of God, or the mood of triumph, when you subjectively feel that you are that which your five senses tell you, you are not; you are then God-intoxicated and seized with a Divine frenzy—a sort of mad joy.

Haven't you at times seen a person bubbling over with enthusiasm and intoxicated with joy? That person is singing the Song of God at that moment. "In thy presence *is* fulness of joy; at thy right hand *there are* pleasures for evermore."

When you sing a song, you are expressing your whole nature. Your mind and body enter into the song. When your heart is full of love and good will, and you are radiating peace, you are truly singing

God's Song; It is the song of the jubilant soul.

The real You is a spiritual, eternal, perfect being. You are a living expression of God now.

"I have said, Ye are Gods; and all of you are children of the most High."

When you pray, it is a romance with God or your Good. Your desire, when realized, brings you joy and peace. In order to realize the desire of your heart, which is depicted in *The Song of Solomon* as your beloved, you must woo it; let that desire of yours captivate, hold, and thrill you. Let it fire your imagination. You will always move in the direction of the desire which dominates your mind.

The majority of students of psychology know that *The Song of Solomon* is a beautiful description of the wonderful romance of the conscious and subconscious mind (Solomon and Sheba).

"Tell me, O thou whom my soul loveth, where thou feedest?" Your realized desire is he whom your soul loveth. You are asked, "Where thou feedest?" In other words what are you mentally dwelling upon? The *flock* represent your thoughts, ideas, opinions, and beliefs. You are to feast on nothing but the joy of the answered prayer.

If you are saying to yourself, "I can't. It is too late now. I am too old, and I don't know the right

people"—in other words if you are mentally feeding on all the reasons why you cannot do something, or be what you want to be, you are not making "thy flock to rest at noon."

At *noon* the sun casts no shadow; likewise, when you pray, you are not to permit any shadow of fear or doubt to cross your path, or deflect you from your goal or aim in life. The world of confusion shall be rejected, and you shall mentally eat of, or meditate on the reality of your desire.

"Behold, thou *art* fair, my love; behold, thou *art* fair; thou *hast* doves' eyes." *The dove* is a symbol of God's inner peace.

Once I talked to an alcoholic who said, "Don't say anything about this God-stuff to me. I don't want God. I want a healing." This man was deeply resentful toward a former wife who had remarried; moreover, he was full of grudges against several people. He needed the *doves' eyes*, which means he needed to see the truth which would give him peace of mind.

I asked him, "Will you pray with me now? All I ask is that you be sincere; if you are, you will experience an inner peace which passeth all human understanding."

He relaxed his body, and I said to him, "Imagine you are talking to the Invisible Presence within you—the Almighty Power which created the Cosmos. It can do

all things. Say, 'Thank you, thank you, for this inner peace.' Say it over and over again."

After ten minutes in silent meditation, he was blinded by an interior, Inner Light. It seemed to come from the floor where he was. The whole room was flooded with Light!

He exclaimed, "All I see is Light! What's wrong?" Then he relaxed into sleep in my office, and his face did truly shine as the sun. He awakened in about fifteen minutes and was completely at peace saying, "God truly is! God is!" This man had found his Beloved; It had *doves' eyes.*

As you fall asleep at night, tell your desire how fair it is, and how wonderful you would feel in realizing it. Begin to fall in love with your ideal. Praise it; exalt it. "Arise my Love!" Feel that you are what you want to be. Go to sleep in the consciousness of being or doing what you long to do.

I told a man in one of the islands one time "to sleep" on the idea of success. He was selling magazine subscriptions. He became a great success by following this procedure: I suggested that he think of success prior to sleep; i.e., what success meant to him; what he would do if he were successful. I told him to use his imagination; then as he was about to go to sleep, fall in love with the idea of success this way: Repeat the one word, "Success," over and over again. He

should get into the mood of success; then fall off to sleep in the arms of his Everlasting Lover. Your Lover —your Divine Presence—will bring to pass whatever you accept as true. The conditions, experiences, and events of your life are called children of your mind.

"He brought me to the banqueting house, and his banner over me *was love.*" The *banquet house* is your own mind where you entertain the idea or desire of your heart.

I will illustrate at this point how to entertain in this *banquet house* of your own mind. A young girl having a special talent to sing was having great difficulty in getting anything to do in the motion picture field, television, or radio. She had been turned down so often she feared she was getting a rejection complex. She heard me state over one of our radio programs that whatever the mind of man could imagine and feel as true, he could realize. She wrote that down; came to one of our classes, and began to practice entering into the banquet house by quieting the wheels of her mind, relaxing the body by simply talking to it, and telling it to relax; it has to obey you. In that quiet, relaxed, peaceful state, with her attention completely focused on an imaginary, movie contract in her hand, she felt the reality of the joy and wonder of it all. She was now in the *banquet house* and the banner over her was love. Love is an emotional attachment. She was definitely, mentally attached to this contract. "He

calleth things that are not seen, as though they were, and the unseen becomes seen." The visible world comes out of the invisible. She caused the contract to become a reality by becoming emotionally attached to the imaginary picture of a contract in her mental, *banquet house.* She knew that what she imagined and believed must come to pass in the three-dimensional world.

"His left hand is under my head, and his right hand doth embrace me." *The left hand* is your deep, subjective feeling; the *right hand* is your disciplined imagination. As you begin to imagine and feel the reality of your desire, you are joining the right and left hands together in a Divine embrace; then a union of the idea and feeling takes place. Another way of saying this is: There is an agreement of the conscious and subconscious mind which denotes the answered prayer.

You know when there is no longer any argument or doubt in your conscious or subconscious mind, your prayer is answered, because the two have agreed as touching upon it, and it is so.

"My beloved spake, and said unto me, Rise up, my love, my fair one, and come away." Is not that what your goal, aim, ambition, or desire is saying to you? For instance the idea of perfect health is now beckoning to you, and saying, "Rise up, and come

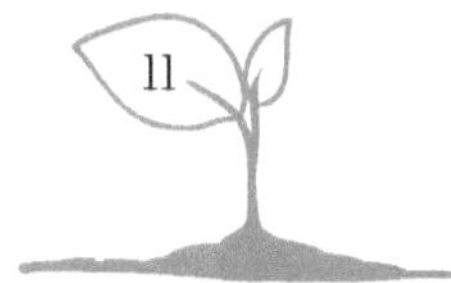

away from the belief in sickness, limitation, pain, and aches to health, harmony, and peace of mind."

I had a long talk with a man in England who had trouble with his leg. He had been confined to his home for nine months and was unable to lean on his leg or walk. The first thing I did was to ask him what he would do if he were healed? He said, "I would again play polo, swim, golf, and climb the alps which I used to do every year." That was the answer I was seeking.

I told him in the simplest way how to achieve the perfect use of his legs again. The first thing was to imagine he was doing the things he would do. I painted an imaginary picture for him. For fifteen or twenty minutes three times a day he sat in his study and imagined he was playing polo; he assumed the mental mood of actually performing the role of a polo player. He became the actor; an actor participates in the role.

Note carefully that he did not see himself playing polo; that would be an illusion. He *felt* himself playing polo. He actualized it by living the drama in his mind or *banquet house.*

At noon he would quiet the mind; still the body, and feel his Alpine clothes on him. He would feel and imagine he was climbing the Alps; he would feel the cold air on his face, and hear the voice of his old associates. He lived the drama and felt the naturalness

and the tangibility of the rocks.

At night prior to sleep, before going into the Arms of his Beloved—His Deeper Self—he would play a game of golf. He would hold the club; touch the ball with his hand; put it in place, and tee off. He would swing his clubs, and delight in watching where the ball went. When he was in the mood of playing a good game, he would go off to sleep feeling very satisfied and happy about his experience.

Within two months this man's leg was healed. He did all the things he imagined he would do. The *idea* of climbing the Alps, plus the *desire* to play polo again, said to this man, "Arise, my love, my fair one, and come away," from your belief in a physical handicap; that is what he did.

The law of the subconscious is one of compulsion. When you subjectively feel you are swimming,—for example, when you feel the chill of the water, and the naturalness of your various swimming strokes,—you will sooner or later be compelled to swim. Whatever the handicap, whether fear or a physical condition, you will do what you subjectively felt you were doing.

Your desire, dream, ambition, goal, or aim is your saviour! It is walking down the corridor of your mind, saying to you, "Arise, my love, and come away," and enjoy the good and glorious things of life.

No matter what the problem is, or its magnitude, you have really nothing to do but convince yourself of the truth which you are affirming. As quickly as you succeed in convincing yourself of the reality of your desire, results will automatically follow. Your subconscious mind will faithfully reproduce what you impregnated within it.

The Bible says, "Choose you this day whom ye will serve." You have the freedom to choose the tone, feeling, or mood you enter into. The manifestation of your feeling or conviction is the secret of your lover or subconscious mind. Your external actions are, therefore, determined by your subconscious beliefs and impressions.

Your thought and feeling determine your destiny. The knowledge of the truth is saying to you now, "The winter is past, the rain is over *and* gone." The *winter* represents that cold state when the seeds are frozen in the bosom of the earth and nothing is growing. The winter and all the seasons are in your mind.

Are your desires, dreams, visions, and aims in life frozen within you due to fear, worry, or false beliefs? You can resurrect them now by turning away from appearances, entering into the *banquet house* of God within you, and saying to yourself, "I can be what I want to be. All I have to do is impress my subconscious mind with my desire for health, wealth,

companionship, or true place, and it will express that state with which I have impressed it.

The *winter* is now over for you; the rain is gone also. Your mind may have been flooded with negative thoughts causing the mood of despondency, dejection, and melancholia. This is what a flood or avalanche of negative thoughts, false beliefs, and erroneous opinions will do. Now you know that all you have to do is fill your mind with the truths of God which have come down to you from time immemorial. As you do this, you will crowd out of your mind everything unlike them.

The winter and the floods are over for you when regularly and systematically you fill your mind with the concept of peace, happiness, love, and good will. You can do this by reading one of the Psalms, such as the twenty-third or ninety-first, and feeling the truth of everything you say; or you can read aloud a good meditation of the real truths of God. As you do this, these truths go in through the eye and the ear; they release a tremendous, therapeutic vibration which courses through your entire mind and body. These curative, healing, soothing vibrations destroy, neutralize, and obliterate all the negative, fearful, diseased thoughts which caused all the trouble in your life; their embodiment must then disappear. This is prayer; do it often enough until it becomes a habit. Prayer should be a habit also.

15

Do everything from the standpoint of the One God and His Love. For instance, when you shop, pray before purchasing. Say, "God guides me in all my purchases." Say quietly to the saleslady or salesman, "God is prospering him."

Whatever you do, do it with love and good will. Pour out love, peace, and good will to all. Claim frequently that God's Love and Transcendent Beauty flow through all my thoughts, words, and actions. Make a habit of this. Fill your mind with the eternal verities; then you will see that "The flowers appear on the earth; the time of the singing of *birds* is come!" You will begin to *flower*; yes, you will begin to blossom forth.

The earth means your body, environment, social life, and all things necessary on this objective plane.

The flowers you witness will be the birth of God in your mind. *The flowers* of God's guidance will watch over you, and lead you to green pastures and still waters. The flowers of God's Love will fill your heart. Now when you see discord anywhere, you will see the Love of God operating in all His Creation; as you realize It, you will see love come forth and flower in the other.

When you go into a home, and you see confusion, quarrelling, and strife, you will realize within yourself, that the peace of God reigns supreme in the

minds and hearts of all those in this house; you will see the flower of peace made manifest and expressed.

Where you see financial lack and limitation, you will realize the infinite abundance and wealth of God forever flowing, filling up all the empty vessels, and leaving a Divine surplus. As you do this, you will live in the garden of God where only orchids and all beautiful flowers grow; for only God's ideas circulate in your mind.

As you go to sleep every night, you will clothe yourself with the garment of love, peace, and joy. From now on you always go to sleep feeling that you now are what you long to be. Your last concept as you fall asleep is etched on your deeper mind; you shall resurrect it. Always take into the *banquet house* of your Lover a noble, Christ-like concept of yourself; your Lover will always give you what you conceive and believe as true. Anything you can conceive, your Lover can give conception. Love gives birth to all things. Your tomorrows are determined by your concept of yourself as you fall asleep in the arms of your Lover (your ideal).

The time of the singing of birds is at hand for you when you cease singing that old song of lack. You have listened to people sing this kind of song: It is like an old gramophone record: "I'm so lonesome; things never went right for me. I never had a chance. I

have been cruelly treated." "I have been operated on three times." "You should hear about all the money I lost." Yes, then they tell about the fear on the lonely road, plus their likes, dislikes, pet peeves, and hates. Imbued with God's love, you will no longer sing that song again. You will sing the new song; for God's ideas and truths (birds) will sing in you.

Then you will *speak in a new tongue* which means the mood of peace, joy, good will, and love. You will no longer react to people and conditions like you did. The Song of God is now heard. Now when someone says something mean or nasty to you, you will immediately transform it by realizing God's peace fills your soul. You will consume it with the fire of right thoughts; the birds will truly sing in your mind and heart as you do. You are happy; you are bubbling over with enthusiasm, and you are looking forward with a joyous expectancy to all good things. Wherever you go, you carry peace with you; all those who come within your orbit are blessed by your inner radiance. You begin to see sermons in stones, tongues in trees, songs in running brooks, and God in everything. *The voice of the turtle* is now heard in your land!

Tennyson said, "Speak to Him thou, for he hears, spirit with spirit shall meet, closer is He than breathing, and nearer than hands and feet."

The voice of the turtle dove is the voice of peace, the

voice of intuition, and of God's inner guidance. You can hear it by lowly listening. For instance one time as a boy I was lost in the woods. I sat down under a tree, and remembered a prayer which starts with, "Our Father, He will shows us the way; let us be quiet, and He will lead us." I quietly repeated, "Father, lead us."

A wave of peace came over me which I can still recall. The voice of the turtle dove became real. *The turtle dove* is intuition which means being taught from within. An overpowering feeling came over me to go in a certain direction as if I were being pushed ahead. Two of the boys came with me; the others did not. We were led out of that thick jungle, as if by an Unseen Hand.

Great musicians have listened and heard the music within; they wrote down what they heard inwardly. In meditation Lincoln listened to the principle of liberty; Beethoven heard the principle of harmony.

If you are intensely interested in the principle of mathematics, you are loving it; as you love it, it will reveal all its secrets to you.

Jesus heard the *voice of the turtle dove* when he said, "Peace, I leave with you; my peace I give unto you; not as the world giveth, give I unto you. Let not your heart be troubled; neither let it be afraid." How wonderful you will feel as you drink in these words and fill your mind with their therapeutic potency.

Job heard *the voice of the turtle* when he said, "Acquaint now thyself with Him, and be at peace." "Thou wilt keep *him* in perfect peace, *whose* mind is stayed *on thee:* because he trusteth in thee." "For God is not *the author* of confusion, but of peace."

You can hear *the voice of the turtle* by turning to the Infinite Intelligence within you, saying, "Father, this is what I want . . ."; then state specifically and clearly the thing you desire. You are now turning your desire over to the God-Wisdom within you, Which knows all, sees all, and has the "know how" of accomplishment. You always know whether you have really turned your request over or not. If you are at peace about it, you have turned it over. If anxious and worried, you have not subjectified your prayer; you do not fully trust the God-Wisdom within.

If you want guidance, claim Infinite Intelligence is guiding you now; It will differentiate Itself as right action for you. You will know you have received the answer, for *the dove of peace* will whisper in your ear, "Peace be still." You will know the Divine answer, for you will be at peace, and your decision will be right.

A girl recently was wondering whether to accept a position in New York for considerably more money or remain in Los Angeles in her present position. At night as she went to sleep, she asked herself this question, "What would be my reaction if I had made

the right decision now?" The answer came to her, "I would feel wonderful. I would feel happy having made the right decision." Then she said, "I will act as though I had made the right decision," and she began to say, "Isn't it wonderful! Isn't it wonderful!" over and over again, as a lullaby, and lulled herself to sleep in the feeling, "It is wonderful."

She had a dream that night, and the voice in the dream said, "Stand still! Stand still!" She awakened immediately, and knew of course that was *the voice of the turtle dove*— the voice of intuition.

The fourth dimensional-self within her can see ahead; it knows all and sees all; it can read the minds of the owners of the business in the east. She remained in her present position. Subsequent events proved the truth of her Inner Voice; the Eastern concern went into bankruptcy. "I the Lord will make myself known unto him in a vision, and will speak unto him in a dream."

"My beloved *is* mine, and I *am* his; he feedeth among *the lilies.*" The lilies represent the poppies which grow in the East. To see the poppy field sway in the breeze is a very beautiful sight. Here the inspired Biblical writer is telling you to have a romance with God. As you turn to the God-Presence, It turns to you. You experience the mystic marriage, the wedded bliss, when you fall madly in love with truth for truth's

sake; then you become full of the new wine, the new interpretation of life.

The lilies symbolize beauty, order, symmetry, and proportion. As you feed or feast on the great truth that God is Indescribable Beauty, Boundless Love, Absolute Bliss, Absolute Harmony, and Infinite Peace, you are truly *feeding among the lil-lies.* When you claim that what is true of God is true of you, miracles will happen in your life.

By realizing and knowing these qualities and attributes of God are being expressed through you, and that you are a channel for the Divine, every atom of your being begins to dance to the rhythm of the Eternal God. Beauty, order, harmony, and peace appear in your mind, body, and business world as you feed among the lilies; you feel your oneness with God, Life, and God's Infinite Riches. You are married to your Beloved, for you are now married to God; you are a bride of the Lord (I AM). From this moment forward you will bring forth children of your Beloved; they will bear the image and likeness of their Father and Mother.

The *father* is God's idea; the *mother* is the emotionalizing of the idea, and it subjective embodiment. From that union of idea and feeling come forth your health, abundance, happiness, and inner peace.

Sit down and feed among the lilies by realizing that every night of the year when you go to sleep, you go before the King of Kings, the Lord of Lords, and the Prince of Peace. Be sure you are dressed properly as you enter into His Holy Presence. If you were going before the President, you would put on your best clothes. The clothes you wear as you enter into the heavens of your own mind every night represent the mood, or the tone you wear. Be sure it is always the wedding garment of love, peace, and good will to all.

Be absolutely sure that you can say, "Behold, thou art fair." There must be no resentment, ill-will, condemnation of self or others, and no criticism of any person. God's Love must really fill your heart for all men everywhere. You must sincerely wish for everyone what you wish for yourself; then you can say to your mood or feeling, "Behold, thou *art* fair." "And when ye stand praying, forgive, if ye have ought against any."

"My beloved is mine." All that God is, is yours, for God is within you. All you can possibly desire is already yours. You need no help from the outside to *feed among the lilies.*

When you go to sleep tonight, forgive everyone, and imagine and feel your desire is fulfilled. Become absolutely and completely indifferent to all thought of failure, because you now know the law. As you

accept the end, you have, as Troward so beautifully stated, willed the means to the realization of the end. As you are about to enter sleep, galvanize yourself into the feeling of being or having your desire. Your mental acceptance or your feeling as you go to sleep is the request you make of your Beloved; then She looks at your request (conviction in the subconscious mind), and being the Absolute Lover, she must give you what you asked.

"You feed among the lilies until the day breaks and the shadows flee away." The shadows are fear, doubt, worry, anxiety, and all the reasons why you cannot do something. The *shadows* of our five senses and race belief hover over the minds of all as we pray.

When you pray, accept as true what your reason and five senses deny and reject. Remain faithful to your idea by being full of faith every step of the way. When your consciousness is fully qualified with the acceptance of your desire, all the fear will go away. Trust in the reality of your ideal or desire until you are filled full of the feeling of being it; then *the day will break and all shadows will flee away.* Yes, the answer to your prayer will come and light up the heavens of your mind bringing you peace.

No matter what the problem is, how acute, dark, or hopeless things seem to be, turn now to God, and say, "How is it in God and Heaven?" The answer will softly

steal over your mind like the dew from heaven: "All is peace, joy, bliss, perfection, wholeness, harmony, and beauty"; then reject the evidence of your senses, and *feed among the lilies of God and Heaven,* such as peace, harmony, joy, and perfection. Realize what is true of God must be true of you and your surroundings. Continue in this abiding trust and faith in God "until the day breaks and the shadows flee away."

THE PRACTICE OF THE PRESENCE OF GOD

"Whither shall I go from thy Spirit? or whither shall I flee from thy presence? If I ascend up into heaven, thou ART THERE, If I take the wings of the morning, AND dwell in the uttermost parts of the sea; Even there shall thy hand lead me, and thy right hand shall hold me."

This one hundred and thirty ninth Psalm is one of the most beautiful Psalms in the Bible. It is a matchless, priceless gem of truth. The language of this Psalm is unsurpassed for beauty and elegance. David's marvelous conception of the Omnipresence of God was found in this passage.

The religion outlined in the Bible is the practice of the Presence of God. To understand and to intelligently practice this truth, you will find is the way to health, harmony, peace, and spiritual progress. The practice of the Presence is powerful beyond imagination. Let us not overlook it, because of its utter simplicity.

The first step is to realize that God is the Only Power. The next thing to become aware of is that all things — no matter what they are — represent God in manifestation. The whole world is God in infinite differentiation, as God never repeats Himself; this is the whole story, and the greatest of all truths. It is really the all-inclusive, all- encompassing truth.

I know many students who sit down for five or ten minutes every day, and meditate on the fact that God is the Only Presence and the Only Power. They let their thoughts dwell on this profound truth; they look at it from all angles; then they begin to think that every person they meet is an expression of God; that in fact everything they see is God made manifest; it is God dramatizing Himself for the joy of expressing Himself. As they do this, they find their whole world changing; they experience better health; outer conditions improve, and they are possessed of a new vitality and energy.

Your whole world will change as you really begin to see God in everything and in everyone. "For thou shalt be in league with the stones of the field: and the beasts of the field shall be at peace with thee. And thou shalt know that thy tabernacle *shall* be in peace." This means that the man who begins to see God everywhere, and who follows and practices the good, will not be afraid of anything. As a matter of fact the whole world will be his friend, and everything will

extend the offer of help whether animate, or what the world calls inanimate.

The only way to magnify the Presence of God in the eyes of others, is to radiate at all times the sunlight of God's Love. Love God or Truth, and you will be under a Divine compulsion for good. You cannot go wrong. You will find that you will never make any real mistake or a wrong choice. Love of all things good, or of the truth, is really the touch of Midas.

In a building the superstructure depends upon the foundation. Let your foundation be God and Him alone. You are always practicing the Presence of God when you activate your mind with true ideas which heal and strengthen you. Your mind needs constant cleansing, disciplining, and direction. By practicing the Presence of God, you are constantly cleansing your mind; this is prayer.

Think all day long from the standpoint of the One God about every person and every situation you meet. Pray at work by realizing God is your partner, and God is in action through all your associates.

Pray driving your car, by realizing the vehicle is God's idea moving from point to point freely, joyously, and lovingly.

Pray when you go into a store by realizing God directs your purchases, that God is prospering the

clerk who waits on you, and that the store is being governed and directed by God's Wisdom.

Let prayer be the orderly, right way of doing everything. Practice the Golden Rule in all your transactions; then you are writing God's Law in your heart.

It is essential for you to get the right concept and understanding of God. Have you meditated? or have you asked yourself what God is? Your concept of God molds, fashions, and shapes your whole future. Your real belief about God is of supreme importance. It is done unto you as you believe. If you say and believe God is the only Presence, the only Power, Infinitely Good, Perfect, Boundless Love, and Limitless Life, your whole life will be transformed.

If you say, "Oh, I do not know what I think of God; my thoughts are confused and muddled," confusion will reign in your life. It does not really matter whether you call God: Reality, Infinite Intelligence, Being, Life, Allah, or Brahma; the real Name of God, in so far as you are concerned, is your concept or your belief about God.

A man said to me one time, "I believe in God, and that is all that matters."

I asked him, "But tell me, what sort of God do you really believe in?"

He said, "I believe in the laws of nature." That was his idea of God, and he cannot transcend this belief. He is subject to that belief, thereby limiting his Inner Powers. He had no idea that God was his own Life, that he could contact this Presence with his thought, that he could be guided, and that he could heal his body by prayer. He was bound by his limited belief about God. Many have said to me that God is some kind of a man in the skies—a sort of a glorified man. Others say and believe there are three persons in God. You will always manifest the result of your belief. If you believe that God is some sort of a tyrannical, inscrutable being living in the skies, ready to judge and punish you for your mistakes and violations of man-made laws and religious taboos, you are bound by that belief, and you cause pain, misery, guilt-complexes, and so forth to follow. This is why Quimby said, "Man is belief expressed."

Your concept of God enters into all departments of your life; it is bound to have its effect upon you. God is Life, and Life seeks to express Itself as Love, Light, Truth, and Beauty. Life cannot wish death, sickness, or disease. To say that Life wishes death would be a violation of its own nature. Life cannot have a tendency toward limitation of any kind. Life is a Oneness, a Wholeness, a Unity, and It seeks to express that Unity in the formed universe.

In order to practice the Presence, you must do the

will of God. What does this mean? *The will of God* must always be the nature of God. You can rest assured the will of God must always be something wonderful and glorious. "His name shall be called Wonderful, Counsellor, The Mighty God, The Everlasting Father, The Prince of Peace."

If your desire, idea, or intention is constructive, if it will bless others, and if it is in keeping with the universal principle of harmony, your will or desire is God's will. Your desire for wealth, true place, abundance, security, and better living conditions conforms to the will or tendency of Life or God.

Life is forever seeking to express Itself through you along higher levels. Enthrone in your mind the concept that God is the Only Presence, the Only Power, and that God is Infinitely Good and Perfect. Think of some of God's qualities and attributes, such as Boundless Love, Infinite Intelligence, Indescribable Beauty, Omnipotence, Omniscience, and Omnipresence. Believe these truths about God, and your whole life will change. You will begin to express more and more Godlike qualities every day. Believe that God is All Life, All Love, All Truth, and All Beauty; accept It in the same way as you accept the sun in the heavens each morning; then you will find a great sense of peace and good will stealing over your mind and heart.

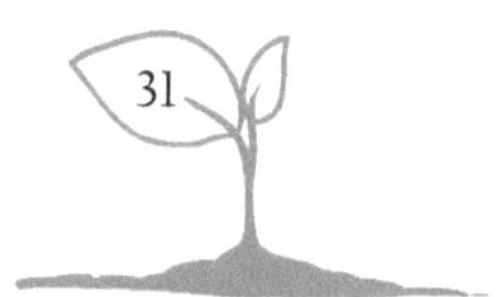

Do you believe in a vengeful, capricious, anthropomorphic Deity who sends sickness, trials, and tribulation to you? Watch the effect of such a belief. If you do, you will be like the man who said to me one time, "God sent this arthritis to me for a good purpose, and I suppose I must just bear it." This is superstition; such an attitude of mind has no foundation. He had arthritis for fifteen years, and he could not overcome it.

When this man with arthritis got a new concept of God, and he learned to forgive those whom he deeply resented, by realizing the Love of God was dissolving in his mind and body everything unlike Itself, he was healed, even though it took some months. This man's concept of God worked out, and made Itself manifest in his body according to his belief.

It is not your theoretical belief about God that manifests itself, but it is your real, deep, subconscious belief.

There are people who forget to practice the Presence when a lawsuit or verdict goes against them. Even though the judge rendered a verdict which seems unjust to you, continue to believe that it is God in action, and that there is a Divine, harmonious solution for all concerned; the matter will come right in due season. You cannot lose; you can only win by practicing the Presence.

If you believe that God is a man in the skies, you must experience the result of such a concept; consequently you experience confusion and trouble, just the same as if some human being with all his whims were running the world.

God is Pure Spirit, Infinite Mind, and Infinite Intelligence. The Bible calls the Name of God, "I AM," meaning Pure, Unconditioned Being. No one can, of course, define God, for God is Infinite, but there are certain Truths which the illumined of all ages have perceived as true of God, and that is why the Bible says, "I AM THAT I AM." What is "I AM?" It is your True Being—your Real Self; nobody can say, "I AM," for you. That is the Presence of God in you, and your Real Identity. Whatever you affix to "I AM," and believe, you become. Always claim, "I am strong, powerful, radiant, happy, joyous, illumined, and inspired"; then you are truly practicing the Presence, for all these qualities are true of God.

When you say, "I am weak," "I am inferior," "I am no good," you are denying God in the midst of you, and lying about Him.

Brother Lawrence of the 17th century was a monk. He was a saintly man, and wholly devoted to God. The book entitled *The Practice of the Presence of God* reveals a great humility, simplicity, and a mystic touch with God. "To do the will of God was," as

he said, "his whole business." Brother Lawrence practiced the Presence when washing the dishes or scrubbing the floor. His attitude was that it was all God's work. His consciousness and awareness of the Divine Presence was no less when employed in the kitchen, than when he was before the altar. The way to God was to Brother Lawrence through the heart and through Love. His superiors marvelled at the man who, though only educated to the point of reading and writing, could express himself with such beauty and profound wisdom. It was the Voice of God within him that prompted all his sayings.

This is how he daily practiced God's Holy Presence: He said in effect, "I have put myself in Your Keeping; it is Your Business I am about, and so everything will be all right." How beautiful! How simple, yet how soul-stirring is this prayer! He said the only sorrow he could experience would be the loss of the sense of God's Presence, but he never feared that, being wholly aware of God's Love and Absolute Goodness.

In his early life he feared he would be damned; this torture of his mind persisted for four years; then he saw the whole cause of this negativity was lack of faith in God; seeing that, he was freed and entered into a life of continual joy.

Brother Lawrence schooled himself whether cooking, baking, or washing pans in the kitchen to

pause, if only for a moment, to think of God in the center of his being, to be conscious of His Presence, and to keep a hidden meeting with Him. Due to his inner illumination, when he enjoyed the raptures of the Spirit, he emerged into a realm of profound peace.

Begin now to practice the Presence by keeping your eyes on God, or all things Good, by seeing God in everyone you meet, and by constantly affirming, "It is God in action in all departments of my life." Calmly trust God's Holy Presence to lead you to green pastures and still waters. Love the Truth with a love that leaves no room for care or doubt. No matter what your work may be, as you go to your business say, "God walks and talks in me. I rely on God's guidance and wisdom completely." Give thanks for the perfect day. Do as Brother Lawrence suggests, whenever your attention wanders away on fear or doubt, bring it back to the contemplation of His Holy Presence.

To secure and know the life of peace and joy, school yourself daily to have an intimate, loving, familiar, humble conversation with God all day long. In this way you will draw upon God's grace abundantly. You shall become illumined by an Inner Light, and you will behold the inner vision of God, your Beloved.

CASE HISTORIES

Case History Number One

This interesting case from my files may bless many of you. This man invested a large sum of money in a certain organization. He had a very high regard for the two men who were active partners in this business. They appropriated the money which he gave them for themselves, and a little later they went into bankruptcy. He was very bitter and resentful, because he had practically put his life's savings into this venture. He was also ill, due to the hatred in his heart.

I explained to this man that resentment is never justified, and that many people make investments in land, stocks, bonds, etc., and have lost their money, but that it is absurd to blame the broker or the real estate man, because we erred in judgment. In a great measure this man's resentment was caused by a feeling of guilt for his own mistake, which he refused to admit. He was blaming the other men by an active resentment for his own shortcoming and failure. He prayed his way through it by the practice of His Presence in this way: "I now radiate love and goodwill to these two men. I humbly, sincerely, and honestly wish for them God's guidance, inner peace, and Divine Love. I wish for each one of them: prosperity, success, and a richness of life. It is God in

action in all departments of their life. I mean this; I am sincere. My mind is now clear, clean, poised, serene, and expectant of happiness. God is guiding me in all ways. Nobody can take happiness, peace, or wealth away from me. I am one with God, and my business is God's Business. I am now minding my own business. The money I gave these men comes back to me in peace and harmony." He prayed like this night and morning, and during the day when hateful thoughts would come, he would say, "God is with me now."

In two weeks he was at peace with the world. All the resentful thoughts were burned up in his deeper mind; they were withered away by realizing God in action in his own life, and the life of those whom he said wronged him. A relative died in the interim, and a most interesting thing happened: He was bequeathed the exact amount he lost in that business venture. "For as the heavens are higher than the earth, so are my ways higher than your ways."

A young girl in our recent Bible Class practiced the Presence in this way: She said, "A man was constantly annoying her by calling her on the phone and meeting her at her place of employment. One day she decided to do something about it. She relaxed; quieted the wheels of her mind; focused all her attention on the God-Presence within by realizing It was there.

She quietly said to herself, "God never made a man like that. Only the God in him is expressed to me. God is all, and only God can be expressed through him." This man completely disappeared out of her life; she never saw him again. She said it was as if the earth swallowed him! Undoubtedly he was healed and blessed by her prayer; she had a healing also.

Prayer always prospers. It is like the gentle rain from heaven; it is twice blessed; it blesses him that gives and him that receives. She saw this man in a new light; then he felt this change within him; he was healed and ceased to annoy her.

"Love your enemies, bless them that curse you, do good to them that hate you, and pray for them which despitefully use you, and persecute you."

REALIZING YOUR DESIRE

Desire is the power behind all action. We could not lift our hand or walk unless we had the desire or urge to move. Desire is the gift of God. As Browning said, "Tis thou, God, who giveth, 'tis I who receive."

It is man who receives—not a few of the gifts of life, but all of them! "Son thou art ever with me, and all that I hath is thine." All things whatsoever the Father hath are mine. *Our Father* holds within Himself all things we require, such as peace, harmony, abundance, guidance, joy, and infinite expression. We must grow unceasingly. We can never exhaust the Infinite Storehouse.

Let us realize a few simple truths: It is due to desire that we jump out of the way of an oncoming bus. The reason we do this is because we have a basic desire to preserve our life. Self-preservation is the first law of nature.

By example, the farmer plants seed due to his desire to attain food for himself and his family. Man builds

airplanes due to his desire to collapse time and space. Similar illustrations are found throughout our whole course of life.

Desire pushes man; it is the goad of action. It is behind all progress. Desire is really the cosmic urge in all of us, impelling us to go forward, onward, upward, and Godward.

Desire is the angel of God—the messenger of the Divine—saying to each one of us, "Come on up higher."

Desire is behind all progress. It is the push of life. We find that we follow the desire which captivates and holds our attention. All of us find ourselves moving in the direction of the idea which dominates our mind for the time being.

Desire is an angel of God, telling us of something which, if accepted by us, will make our life fuller and happier. *The greater the expected benefit from the desire, the stronger is our desire.* Where there is no expected benefit, gain, or advancement accruing, there is no desire; consequently no action is found.

"I am alpha and omega, the beginning and the end, saith the Lord." Our ideal murmuring in our hearts is the alpha; in order that it become the omega, we must enter into the feeling that it is ours now, and walk the earth knowing that it is so.

Failure to realize our desire over a long period of time results in frustration and unhappiness. I have talked to many men in different parts of the country; their frequent complaint is that for years they have tried in vain to attain a certain ideal or position in life, and that they have failed miserably. They did not know that the desire to be, to do, and to have was the Still Small Voice speaking to them, and all that was necessary was for them to say, "Yes, Father, I accept and believe it"; then walk the earth knowing that, "It is done."

By illustration take the seed which draws all that it requires, such as water, chemicals, etc. from the ground, and when it comes above the ground, it extracts from the rays of the sun through a process of photosynthesis all the light and other elements necessary to form a complex substance called chlorophyll. It also has the intelligence within it to make the most complex, chemical compounds in its bark and leaves beyond the ken of man to discover.

In like manner when man becomes as the seed, and knows that all things necessary for the unfoldment of his ideal will be given to him, he will attract to himself whatsoever things he needs for the complete realization of his dream, for instance: friends, funds, introductions, ideas, etc.

All men, women, and children that help us on the

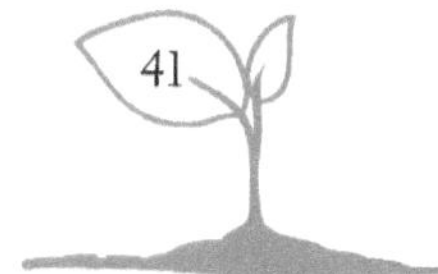

road of life are servants of the law which we set in operation within us. "My ways are not your ways." This Infinite Intelligence, which we set in motion when we pray aright, inspires in others the actions, words, and movements necessary to aid us in the grand unfoldment of our ideal or in the great drama of our life.

It is foolish to blame or accuse others, as we must realize that others are witnesses telling us who we are—"As within, so without." If there is discord within, there will be discord without. If we dwell in a mood of lack and limitation, others must come and testify to our lack.

I knew a woman in London one time, and on three occasions her purse was snatched from her by a thief in the tube of London; she was a wealthy woman. The explanation for this is that she was living in the fear of having her purse stolen; this was really an expectancy. "What I fear most has come upon me."

The mood, feeling, or conviction in which we walk determines the movements and actions of others toward us. In the eleventh chapter of Mark it says, "All things whatsoever ye shall ask in prayer, believe that ye receive them, and ye shall receive them."

The word *whatsoever* in the above quotation means anything you wish; it is all inclusive. There are no specific conditions set forth; you do not have to be

a church-goer, or belong to a certain creed, or make any sacrifices. "I rejoice not in the sacrifices of man, not by power, not by might, but by the spirit saith the Lord." "For what purposes is the multitude of thy sacrifices. I am full of the blood of rams and the fat of beast, I rejoice not in the blood of rams or he goats." The only requisite is to believe that you have it now, or that you are the being you long to be.

Believe means to live in the state of being it; this means a complete mental acceptance where there is no longer any doubt or question in your mind. This is the state of consciousness called "a conviction." All other procedures as cited by Isaiah are foolishness and superstition. The only prerequisite is to believe that you have received; then comes the manifestation of your ideal.

We grow through desire. It is desire that pushes us forward, for it is the cosmic urge.

Let us realize that we are all channels of the Divine—individualizations of God-consciousness. The desire that lingers in your heart, that murmurs quietly—perhaps it has been there for months making itself known to you—is the Voice of God speaking to you, telling you to come on up higher—to arise and shine. Maybe you have looked around you and said to yourself, "What chance have I?" "Mary can, but I can't." "Perhaps, someday!" "It is just wishful

thinking, etc." Have many such expressions come to your mind? Remember it is your five senses and worldly reason arguing with your Higher Self. We must remember that in prayer we always shut out the evidence of our senses and reason, plus everything that contradicts or denies what we truly want; then, as Jesus commands, we go within; shut the door, and pray to our Father in secret; the Father who seeth in secret will reward thee openly. Let us now proceed to enter into this Secret Place, and perform the spiritual, creative act in our own mind.

Sit down in an armchair, relax, and let go. Practice the Nancy School technique by getting into a drowsy, meditative state, a state of effortless effort, wherein effort is reduced to a minimum.

By example if you want to be a singer on the radio, imagine you are before a microphone; the microphone is now in front of you, and you see the imaginary audience; you are the actor. ("Act as though I am, and I will be.") You *feel* yourself into the situation; you are singing now (in your imagination); enter into the joy of it; feel the thrill of accomplishment! Continue to do this in your imagination until it begins to feel natural for you; then go off to sleep. If you have succeeded in planting your desire in your subconscious mind, you will feel a great sense of peace and satisfaction when you awaken. An interesting thing will have happened: You will have no further desire to pray about it,

because it is fixed in consciousness. The reason for this is that the creative act has been finished, and you are at rest.

After true prayer when you have reached an inner conviction, there steals over you a sense of inner peace, calm, and certitude which tells you, "All is well." This is called *the sabbath* in the Bible, or period of stillness, or rest; it is the interval that elapses between the subjective realization of your desire and its manifestation. The manner of manifestation is not known to you; that is the secret of the subjective. "My ways are past finding out."

The answer or manifestation comes as a thief in the night. You know a thief comes when you least expect him; there is always an element of surprise; perhaps when you are sound asleep, the thief will come. If you sit up watching and waiting for the intruder, he will not come. Likewise we must go about our daily business, and the moment we think not, the answer will come. You are now at peace, made whole so to speak. You do not have to assist this Infinite Intelligence; It is All Powerful. It would be foolish to try to add power to Power.

The trouble with many people is this: When they pray, they are tense, anxious, and impatient. They say, "I wonder when it will come?" Others say, "Why has it not happened yet?"

If I say, "Why?" it means I am anxious and lack faith. If I *know* a thing is true, I do not question my prayer. Let us remember, therefore, anytime we ask, "Why?" to ourself or another, it means we have not reached a conviction within ourselves.

When we possess something in consciousness, we do not seek it; we have it! Another point I want to stress here is: When the student questions, "How will it come?" he shows lack of faith and conviction.

By illustration, I am now in Los Angeles, I do not ask, "How will I get there?" I am there. Similarly when our ideal is fixed in consciousness, we do not wonder, "How will I get there?" I am there already. Where your consciousness is, you are. "Where I am there you will be also."

CASE HISTORY

Case History Number One

Several years ago the author was lecturing in the Park Central Hotel in New York City. A man spoke to me at the end of the meeting saying, "I desire desperately to go to Pittsburgh, and I have no money."

I said to him, "Did you hear the lecture?"

He said, "Yes, but—"

I told him to ignore the doubts in his mind. We made a simple statement of truth together in that

46

lovely, lecture room. The statement was, "I am now at home in Pittsburgh with my people. All is peace and harmony." He was at home with them during those few minutes of silence in his imagination and feeling.

He phoned me later saying, "I went to the restaurant, and a man who sat next to me said, "You know I am driving to Pittsburgh. I would love to have someone share in the driving; I would pay him also. Do you know anyone? You look like a mechanic." This was the way Infinite Intelligence answered this man's prayer.

Case History Number Two

I want to tell you of another experience I had in the army. A young soldier said to me, "You know before the war I tried to get into Bellevue Medical School for several years; I was always turned down; yet my marks were very high."

This boy believed he was a victim of racial prejudice. He was attached to my battalion. We chatted one night about the laws of life. I discussed with him the relationship of the conscious and subconscious mind which is given in detail in my book, *The Miracles of Your Mind*. I explained to him that his subconscious mind had the answer; it knew all, and had the "know how" of accomplishment.

I reviewed with him some experiments that I had

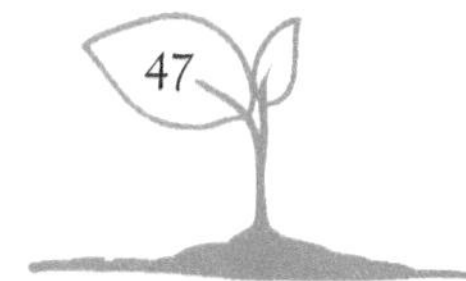

conducted several years previously with a refugee Psychologist from Berlin. In one instance a boy under these experiments became clairvoyant and described things taking place at a distance, which we subsequently verified. This boy also gave the location of missing articles and predicted accurately certain international incidents. We discussed the fact that Infinite Intelligence and Wisdom is lodged in the subliminal mind of man; it is possible to tune in with It, and to get It to work for us.

Accordingly and apropos to the above conversation, the following experiment was suggested to him: "At night as he was about to fall asleep, he would imagine he saw a medical diploma inscribed with his name stating he was a physician and surgeon. He felt this diploma with his hand and imagined the joy of it all. He made it real and natural by focusing his attention on one thing—the diploma—the finished thing; then he contemplated the reality of it.

"Believe that you have it now, and ye shall receive it." "Call things that be not, as though they were, and the unseen becomes seen." "I told you before it came to pass, that when it is come to pass, ye might believe." These are perfect formulas for prayer.

This boy went to the end; he asked himself this question: "What actually would I receive to prove to the world that I am a doctor?" The answer came, "A

diploma!" In his imagination, he saw the diploma and made it real. He went to sleep feeling the diploma in his hand.

By example, you can close your eyes now and feel silk, mohair, or a fur coat on you.

As you feel the naturalness of the fur coat, you will receive it.

The sequel to this soldier's prayer is very interesting: This man said to me one morning, "You know I have a feeling that something is going to happen, and that I won't be around here long." This was the subconscious mind telling him, "All is well."

We know sometimes by a hunch, an inner awareness, or feeling that our prayer is answered. Technically we would say the idea has been sub-subjectified or embodied in the subconscious. In truth we would say the soldier accepted the idea in consciousness, and his inner knowing brought it to pass. The many words or phrases we use all illustrate the same thing, namely, he felt the reality of it; that is all that is necessary. The technique he used aided him in its fulfillment.

The commanding officer called him in and informed him that in view of his pre- medical training, he was to take an examination; if he received good marks, he would be sent to the Medical College at the expense

of the Army. It ensued that he was sent to Stanford, and not to Bellevue. "My ways are past finding out." (It had been explained to him that he did not have to go to Bellevue to be a doctor; let Infinite Intelligence be the guide.)

In prayer go to the end. Feel that you are now what you desire to be; then Infinite Intelligence takes charge, and acts on the thoughts, ideas, and actions of others, so that they aid us in the realization of our desire. (In the same manner a seed attracts to it all things, such as chemicals, water, sunshine, air, etc., necessary for its growth.)

We are always using this Principle, Power, Intelligence, and Wisdom all the days of our life. When we lift our hand to write, we use this Power and Energy. In the same manner when we breathe, we are using the same air.

For example, I am writing now. The ideas expressed come from the One Mind, common to all individual men. There is only One Source, and That is God. We do not originate anything; for all ideas live, move, and have their being in God. This Infinite Being, Consciousness, Awareness, or whatever we choose to call It is the only Originator—the Fountain of all. All men drink from this One Source or Spring. You will understand from these truths that when we look at the sun or a tree, we all see a sun and a tree,

which shows that all of us are using the One Mind.

There is, therefore, no such thing as an atheist; there could not be, because he is using the Mind, the Power, and the Intelligence which is of God. He is alive, and the very Life of him is God, for God is Life. When he says, "I do not believe in God," you can see how absurd it is. He knows, and he believes, he is alive. Aliveness, Awareness is God.

As a teacher I wish to point out that there is no teacher who could give you anything new; he could not; neither can he give you truth. All any teacher can do is to awaken that which is already within you. You house God. As the Book of Revelation says, "The tabernacle of God is with man." A teacher causes you to see the truth which was always there; he kindles a fire if he is a good teacher; then you warm yourself by its glow. But the fire, the glow, and the warmth, thereof, were always within you. The real teacher, if he has a good knowledge of truth, will teach you freedom, and tell you frankly that you do not owe him any allegiance, since your heart belongs to God or the Truth. "To thine own self be true, as the night the day, thou canst then be false to no man." The teacher of truth will tell you if you do not get anything from him, to go elsewhere where you will be blessed. We call our own; there is no competition in truth.

You do not have to strive toward a goal; for the goal you seek already is, and through your treatment work you appropriate it by accepting the state desire in consciousness. All states coexist in the Greater Now, or other dimensions of your mind. It is like the keyboard of a piano; the music you wish to play is already in the piano; all you do is to strike the proper keys and chords to bring it forth, but the tune or the sonata was always there; you do not create it. All you did was to recognize a certain composition and to bring it forth. You can play on the piano *Pop Goes The Weasel or a Beethoven Sonata;* the piano does not care.

Similarly look at the English alphabet; you did not create it; it always existed in Infinite Mind. With this alphabet you can write a beautiful, magnificent drama of life, or you may write a gossip column that may cause some misguided person to commit suicide.

We must strike the key to bring forth our music also; our music is: harmony, health, peace, true place, or expression in life. We strike the proper key by contemplating the reality of the state sought now, feeling, and believing ourselves to possess it.

A simple illustration is as follows: Suppose you wish to sell a home for $20,000. This is the price you would pay for it if the tables were reversed. You are satisfied this is the correct price, and there is no

quarrel in your consciousness. The next step is, as Troward says, "to see the end." A simple way to do this is to take a little phrase that is easily graven on the memory, for instance, "It is sold," or "It is done," and repeat it over and over again like a lullaby until you feel the naturalness and reality of it. (This latter procedure is suggested by the New Nancy School. See Bau-douin's Book, *Auto-Suggestion.*)

The author has instructed many people in the sale of property as follows: See the check in your hand, and feel the joy of accomplishment. Imagining that you have the check in your hand is seeing the end, and having seen the end as Troward says, you have willed the means to the realization of the end. Infinite Spirit will attract to you the person who wants what you have to offer; the price and the time will be right, and you will find the place will be sold in peace and harmony for all concerned. "Let him that is athirst come and drink of the waters of life freely."

THE MAGIC OF FAITH

The purpose of this chapter is to teach you the spiritual truth of your dominion and freedom. "In all thy ways acknowledge him, and he shall direct thy paths." (Prov. 3:6). "I will lift up mine eyes unto the hills, from whence cometh my help." (Psm. 121:1).

In the above verse from proverbs you are told to acknowledge the Infinite Intelligence within you, and that It shall direct you in all ways. The answer to your problem will come when you turn in faith and recognition to the Divine Principle within.

It was Shakespeare who said, "Our doubts are traitors, making us lose the good we oft might win, by fearing to attempt." Fear holds us back. *Fear* is a lack of faith in God or the Good.

A man told me one time that he was a member of a sales force for a large, chemical organization which had two hundred men in the field. The sales manager died, and the vice president offered him the position; however he turned it down. He realized later that

54

the only reason he rejected the offer was due to fear. He was afraid to attempt the responsibility. This man lacked faith in himself and his Inner Power. He hesitated, and the wonderful opportunity passed him by.

This salesman came to me for consultation, and I learned he was condemning himself, which was like a destructive, mental poison. In place of condemnation, he began to realize there were other opportunities. I explained to him that faith is a way of thinking, a positive mental attitude, or a feeling of confidence that what you are praying for will come to pass.

For example, you have faith that the sun will rise tomorrow. You have faith that the seed you deposited in the ground will grow. The electrician has faith that electricity will respond to his proper use of it. A scientist has an idea for an ediphone; he proceeds to bring it to pass by having faith in the execution of the invisible idea.

Opportunity is always knocking at your door. The desire for health, harmony, peace, and prosperity is knocking at your door now. Perhaps you are offered a promotion; are you going to act like Peter of old who walked on the waters? ("And when Peter was come down out of the ship, he walked on the water, to go to Jesus. But when he saw the wind boisterous, he was afraid; and beginning to sink, he cried, Lord, save me.")

Besides being historical, this drama of Peter and Jesus takes place in your own mind. *Peter* means faith, perseverance, and determination. Jesus means your desire which, if realized, would be your saviour. Jesus comes into your mind as an idea, desire, plan, purpose, vision, or some new undertaking. The realization of your dreams, plans, or purpose would bring you and others great satisfaction and inner joy; this would be your Jesus. You must now call Peter which is faith in the God-Power to bring all things to pass. Look at Peter and Jesus as dramatizations of the power of truth within you.

Oftentimes as you attempt something new,— for example, a new position,—doubt comes into your mind; this is Peter in you looking at the *boisterous wind and sinking.* This represents the impingement in your mind of the race belief in failure, lack, and limitation.

You must cremate, burn up, and destroy that negative thought immediately. You must not suffer a witch to live; meaning you must supplant the negative feeling with the positive thoughts of success, peace, and prosperity immediately, and give your love and feeling to these concepts. As you sustain this mood of confidence, you will become victorious.

Doubt and fear hold men in bondage of sickness and failure. These false concepts cause you to vacillate, waver, equivocate, and hesitate to go ahead.

The way to overcome is to increase your faith and awareness of your deep, spiritual potencies. Be like Peter; he succeeded, because he went forward; he had faith and confidence, knowing he would succeed.

A general in the field cannot afford to vacillate and waver on the battlefield. He has to come to a decision. Failure to come to a decision, plus a constant wavering in the mind, leads to a nervous breakdown and mental confusion. When you find yourself being pulled two ways, that is a sign of doubt and fear.

Your good comes to you in the form of your desire. If you are sick, you wish health. If you are poor, you desire wealth. If you are full of fear, you desire faith and confidence. Jesus comes as your desire walking down the streets of your mind.

There is another part of your mind which says, "No, it can't be. It is too late now." "It is impossible." This is the time to lift up your eyes unto the hills from whence cometh your help; i.e., you lift up your eyes when you focus your attention on your good. Remember faith can do all things. "Thy faith hath made thee whole." "According to your faith is it done unto you." You must appreciate the fact that your desire, idea, or dream is real, though it is invisible. To know that the idea is real, that it is a fact of consciousness, gives you faith, and enables you to move over the waters of confusion, strife, and fear to

a place of conviction deep in your own heart. Peter said, "Lord, if it be thou, bid me come unto thee on the water."

Ideas are our lords and masters. Ideas govern and rule us. The dominant idea which you now entertain is your lord; it generates its own emotion. Emotions compel you to express them. The dominant idea of success enthroned in the mind generates its own mood or feeling. This feeling compels you to right action, so that whatever you do under the mood of faith and confidence will be successful. The desire or idea of yours now is your lord. "Lord, if It be thou, bid me come to thee upon the water." Mentally appropriate your desire, kiss it, love it, let it captivate your mind; feel the reality of it.

Is your desire lofty, inspiring, and wonderful enough to lead you forward? This ideal of yours is real, just the same as the idea of a radio was real in the mind of the inventor; or the idea of an automobile was real in the mind of Ford; or the idea of a house is real in the mind of an architect. It is not idle fancy or a daydream.

Peter is within you; i.e., *Peter* is faith, perseverance, stick-to-it-iveness, and an abiding trust in an Almighty Power which responds to man's thought and belief. This Formless Awareness within you takes the form of your belief and conviction. It is

really all things to all men. It is strength to you, if you need strength. It is guidance, if you need guidance. It is food and health also.

Everyone has faith in something. What is your faith? Let it be faith in all things good, a joyous expectancy of the best, and a firm belief inscribed in your heart that Infinite Intelligence will lead you out of your difficulty, and show you the way. You have a firm conviction now in the Power of God to solve your problems and heal you. This faith in God enables you to walk over all the waters of fear, doubt, worry, and imaginary dangers of all kinds. You now know that error and fear are false beliefs without power. You know these negative states are false and groundless. Paul says, "Faith is the substance of things hoped for, the evidence of things not seen." It is from faith or feeling that all things flow.

When you look down, you see mud, but when you look up, you see the stars! Similarly, when you say, "There is no way out. I have no chance," you are looking like Peter at the winds of confusion, fear, and human opinion; but when he remembers where his power is, he *looks up at Jesus*, meaning that he looks at the solution, the way out, the happy ending, and ignores the winds of human intellect and the waves of race mind.

The man of faith puts his trust in the Invisible

Power within him. He knows this is the Kingdom of the Real. He knows that his ideal is real in the Inner Kingdom, and that his faith or feeling will cause the formless or the invisible to take on form as a condition, event, or experience. This is why the man of faith walks upon the waters, and moves in confidence and understanding to the promised land—his cherished goal. Faith is accepting as true what your reason and intellect deny.

All great scientists, mystics, artists, poets, and inventors are gifted or possessed by an abiding faith and trust in the Invisible Powers within.

Faith is trust. You trusted your mother when you were in her arms; you looked into her eyes, and you saw love there. Your *Peter* is your faith and trust in God, the Absolute Lover, and it should be greater than faith in your mother.

As you read this, turn your desire or request over to the subjective mind within you, acknowledging in your heart it has the answer and the "know how" of accomplishment, and that its ways are past finding out. When you are relaxed and peaceful, you will know you have succeeded in impregnating your deeper mind. Signs follow; the wave of peace is the sign; this is inner conviction. You now walk above all the waters of confusion, chaos, and false beliefs, because in a little while what you felt as true will be

60

experienced.

Troward says if a thing is true, there is a way in which it is true. Look at the magic and miracle-working power of faith in your own life. Behold the miracle which takes place as you drink a glass of milk; it is transformed into tissue, muscle, bone, hair, and blood cells in your body by the Master Chemist within. Look within for your saviour. Your true saviour is your thought and feeling. Blend these together, and you have a holy covenant, a wedded bliss, the mystic marriage. Any idea or desire impregnated with love is invincible; this is working faith. Blend Peter (faith) and Jesus (desire) together, and the miracle will happen.

CASE HISTORIES

Case History Number I

I visited a man in prison a few months ago. The first thought in his mind was freedom; this is symbolized in the Bible as Jesus walking on the waters of your mind. This prisoner was very bitter and cynical. I explained to him that he had placed himself in prison by his actions which were contrary to the golden rule. He was living in a psychological prison of hatred and envy. He changed his mental attitude by calling forth Peter which was his faith in an Almighty Power to bring to pass the cherished desire of his heart.

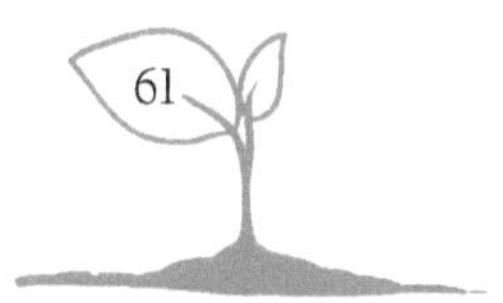

I gave detailed instruction to this prisoner. He began to pray for those he hated by saying frequently, "God's love flows through them, and I release them." He began to do this many times a day. At night prior to sleep, he imagined himself home with his family. He would feel his little daughter in his arms and hear her voice saying, "Welcome, daddy." All this was done in his imagination. After awhile he made this so real, natural, and vivid, that it became a part of him. He had impregnated the subconscious with the belief in freedom.

Another interesting thing happened; he had no further desire to pray for his freedom; this was a sure psychological sign to him that he had embodied the desire for freedom subjectively. He was at peace, and though he was behind bars, he knew subjectively that he was free. It was an inner knowing. You no longer seek that which you have. Having realized his desire subjectively, he had no further desire to pray about it.

A few weeks passed by, and this young man was liberated from prison. Friends came to his rescue, and through the proper channels, the door was opened to him for a new life.

Case History Number Two

A student in our Bible class stated that there was no way to save her boy-friend from losing his store. He could not meet the bills; even his automobile was attached.

She was saying, "It isn't possible. I see no way out. It is just hopeless." She listened to one of our lectures on prayer and applied it that night.

She said, "I will walk upon the waters of doubt and negativity, and 'I will say of the Lord, He is my refuge, and my fortress: my God; in him will I trust.' " She anchored her mind on the following great truth: "God's peace floods his mind, and God answers him."

She remained in a quiet, passive state; she got into the mood or feeling that there was a solution for her boy-friend, and went off to sleep, dwelling on the following, wonderful words of truth: "I stand still, and I see the salvation of the Lord." This young girl knew that the saviour was in her own faith; she turned her eyes to the hills; these *hills* are always of an inner range; they are the hills of faith and trust in God which moves mountains. Reject mentally all sense-evidence, and look into the eyes of your saviour; this means to live in the emotional embodiment of your desire or ideal.

The following day her boy-friend called her and told her that a miracle had happened. A check was presented to him the following day for $2,000 by a man who had borrowed this amount ten years previously. It came out of the blue as a perfect response to her prayer of faith.

STEPS TO HAPPINESS

Happiness is a state of consciousness. Faith and fear are moods of the soul. Your faith is a joyous expectancy of the best. Fear comes to challenge your faith in God or the Good. You must look upon fear as man's ignorance or his false beliefs which try to overcome his conviction in the good.

Never entertain or accept the suggestions of sickness, weakness, or failure. If you listen to negative suggestions and become fearful, begin to affirm the Truths of God, such as Love, Peace, Joy, etc. Know that thought and feeling are the causes of conditions and experiences.

Fear is based on the false beliefs that there are other powers, and that external things and conditions can hurt you. Fear must leave you, because it has nothing to sustain it; there is no reality behind it; its claims are false. Come back to the simple truth: "Only your thought has power over you, and the One Almighty Power now moves on your behalf, because your

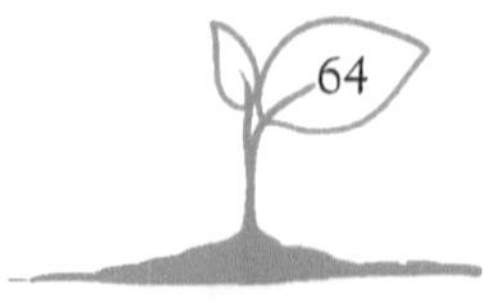

thoughts are in tune with the Infinite One.

The man full of faith in God is never concerned about the future. When worry or fear knock at the door of his mind, faith in God opens the door, and he is at peace.

I met a farmer one time on the west coast of Ireland. I lived in his house for a few days. He seemed to be always happy and joyful. I asked him to tell me his secret of happiness. His answer was, "It is a habit of mine to be happy." This is the whole story! Prayer is a habit; happiness is likewise a habit.

> There is a phase in the Bible which says, "Choose ye this day whom ye will serve." You have the freedom *to choose* happiness; this may seem extraordinarily simple—and it is. Perhaps this is why people stumble over the way to happiness; they do not see the simplicity of the key to happiness. You can choose unhappiness by entertaining these ideas: "Today is a black day; everything is going to go wrong." "I am not going to be successful." "Everyone is against me."

Perhaps you say to yourself, "Business is bad. It is going to get worse." Furthermore, you may say to yourself, "The worst is yet to come!" If you have this attitude of mind the first thing in the morning, you will attract all these experiences to you, and you will be very unhappy.

On the other hand you can choose happiness. This is how you do it: When you open your eyes in the morning, say to yourself, "All things work together for good to them that love God." Remember that in all languages God and Good are synonymous.

Love is an emotional attachment. Continue to become attached to the good in the morning in this way: Look out the window, and say, "This is God's day for me. I am Divinely guided all day long. Whatever I do will prosper. I cast the spell of God around me. I walk in His Light. Whenever my attention wanders away from God or the Good, I will immediately bring it back to the contemplation of God and His Holy Presence. I am a spiritual magnet attracting to myself all things which bless and prosper me. I am going to be a wonderful success in all my undertakings today. I am definitely going to be happy all day long."

Start each day in this manner; then you are choosing happiness, and you will be a radiant, joyous person.

You can experience nothing outside your own mentality. Your dominant, mental mood is the way you think and feel inside about yourself, others, and the world in general. What is your present mental attitude? How do you feel inside? Are you worried, confused, angry, or concerned about other people's actions? If you are, you are not happy, because you are dwelling mentally on limitation.

Begin to anchor your mind on thoughts of peace, success, and happiness; this is really prayer. Do this frequently; then you will be like the Irish farmer who said, "It is a habit of mine to be happy." Your dominant mental attitude rules and governs all your experiences; therefore nothing can come into your world but the out-picturing of your mental attitude. Love all things good, and even your so-called "enemies" will be constrained to do you good.

Oftentimes you read in psychological and metaphysical literature that the world you behold is the world you are; this means you can control your relationship with the world. The world you really live in is a mental world of thoughts, feelings, sensations, and beliefs. As a matter of fact every person, circumstance, and experience you meet becomes a thought in your mind. How you mentally feel and react to life and conditions depend on what you believe about life and things in general. If your knowledge about life and the world is false, you can be very unhappy. If you have true knowledge and the right ideas, you can control your emotional reactions to life and have inner peace.

You are now awakening to the truth that happiness is determined by what goes on in your mind. There is one very important point about being happy: You must sincerely *desire* to be happy. There are people who have been depressed, dejected, and unhappy so

long, that were they suddenly made happy by some wonderful, good, joyful news, they would actually be like the woman who said to me, "It is wrong to be so happy!" They have been so accustomed to the old, mental patterns that they do not feel at home being happy! They long for the former, depressed, unhappy state.

I knew a woman in England who had rheumatism for twenty years. She would pat herself on the knee, and say, "My rheumatism is bad today. I can't go out; my rheumatism keeps me miserable." This dear, elderly lady got a lot of attention from her son, daughter, and the neighbors. She really wanted her rheumatism; she enjoyed her "misery," as she called it. This person did not really want to be happy.

I suggested a curative procedure given in the Bible. I wrote down some biblical verses, and said if she gave her attention to these truths, she would be healed, but she was not interested. There seems to be a peculiar, mental streak in many people, whereby they seem to enjoy being miserable and sad.

Jesus said, "If you know these things, happy are ye if ye do them." "We should become as little children." The reason for this is that a child is happy, because it is close to God. The child knows intuitively where to find happiness. You do not have to become old, dull, crotchety, petulant, and cantankerous; neither

do you have to become jaded and depressed in spirit. The simple truths of life, and not the opinions of man, produce and generate happiness within us. There are a great number of people trying to buy happiness through the purchase of radios, television sets, automobiles, and a home in the country, but happiness can not be purchased or procured that way.

The Kingdom of God is within you, and the kingdom of happiness is in your thought and feeling. Too many people have the idea that it takes something artificial to produce happiness. Some people say, "If I had a million dollars, I would be happy." Others say, "If I was elected mayor, or the president of the organization, I would be happy." The answer is, "We must *choose* happiness." We must make it a habit to be happy. It is a mental and spiritual state. Happiness comes through your daily visits with God and in silent communion with His Holy Presence.

Begin now to eat the bread of the silence; you do this by meditating on the fact that, "In Him there is fullness of joy." As you dwell on these words, imagine the joy and the love of God are flowing through your mind and heart as a living current or stream; then you are stirring up the gift of God within you.

The Saviour is within you, but He is asleep. Awaken Him! It takes only thought to stir God into

action. Every time you mentally reject the power of conditions and circumstances and recognize the Presence of God in you, you are stirring up the gift of God within you. "Wherefore I put thee in remembrance that thou stir up the gift of God, which is in thee."

When your mind is clean and wholesome, when your eyes are dedicated and focused on God or the Good, and when you have a child's heart, your mind is at peace; then you are full of good will, and you are happy.

Say to yourself every day when you awaken, "God is my partner." If the day is raining, say with joy, "How wonderful it is to see God in action!" When you see snow falling, give thanks. When the sun shines, know it is blessing everyone.

Within you is the Power to overcome any situation. You were born to win, to succeed, and to conquer. There is a great thrill in mastering a difficult assignment; the joy is in overcoming. Stand up against the problem now. Take up that shining sword of truth, and say, "I go forth conquering and to conquer!" The Power of the Almighty is within you; It will reveal to you the perfect solution. It will show you the way you should go. Conquer and overcome every negative emotion within you. Love casts out fear. The peace of God casts out pain. Good will casts

out envy. In the midst of all kinds of adversity, look for that which is good, and that which is right; in other words look for the Divine answer.

Turn within you now and say, "Every morning I will say, 'There is something happy on my way.'" Evil has no reality; for your evil is your disorganized mind.

God is Life, and Life is forever seeking to express Itself in ways of pleasantness and paths of peace. Its tendency is Lifeward. The urge of Life is progression. Life is seeking to express through you as harmony, health, peace, joy, and happiness; these are the truths you are seeking. There is nothing but Good in God's universal, cosmic design. Enthrone in your mind the thought of the complete Omnipotence of God, and that God is watching over you, guiding you in all your ways. Let your mind be imbued with this idea, and the waters of healing will flow through you. As you focus your attention on these truths, you are making it a habit to be happy.

CASE HISTORIES

Case History Number One

I knew an alcoholic in London who had sunk to the depths of degradation. When I met him, he was begging pennies on the street for drink. At one time he was a highly respected lawyer. I spent some time with him in Hyde Park, London, telling him a few

simple truths. I wrote these words for him to repeat: "I surrender myself completely to God and His Boundless Love and Goodness. My mind and heart are now open to the Spirit of Almighty God which flows through me now. God fills my mind and heart with His Joy and His Love. I do not see the wind, but I feel the breeze upon my face; likewise I feel God's Presence stirring in my heart. God's river of Love flows through me, and I am clean and made whole."

I told him to relax, and slowly articulate the above meditation fifteen minutes, three times a day. All that was necessary was sincerity and humility on his part; then he was assured he would be free from the habit and blessed beyond his wildest dreams. This man became childlike in his simplicity. He fulfilled his promise. In less than a week he was engaged in a romance with God. Truly he touched the hem of His garment. As he meditated aloud, he imagined that the words were seeds sinking down into his soul. On the sixth day his whole being and his room were flooded with an Interior Light which seemed to blind him temporarily. He was completely healed.

Case History Number Two

Lecturing in San Francisco some years ago, I interviewed a man who was very unhappy and dejected over the way his business was going. He was the general manager. His heart was filled with

resentment toward the vice president and the president of the organization; "They opposed him," he claimed. Because of this internal strife, business was declining; he was receiving no dividends.

This is how he prayed and solved his business problems: The first thing in the morning, he used the following meditation, "All those working in our corporation are spiritual, wonderful, Godlike links in the chain of its growth, welfare, and prosperity. I radiate good will in my thoughts, words, and deeds to my two associates and all those in the company. God's Love and good will fill my heart for the president and the vice president of our company. Infinite Intelligence and Divine Wisdom make all decisions through me. There is only right action taking place in our life. I send the messengers of peace, love, and good will before me to the office, and the peace of God reigns supreme in the minds and hearts of all those in the company including myself. I now go forth into a new day full of faith, confidence, and trust."

This business executive repeated the above meditation slowly three times in the morning feeling the truth behind the words. He put life, love, truth, and beauty into the words, and they went deep down into his subconscious mind. When fearful or angry thoughts came into his mind during the day, he would say, "God is within me now." After awhile all the harmful thoughts ceased to come, and peace came

into his mind. He wrote me in New York saying that at the end of the two weeks, the president and the vice president called him into the office, apologized, and shook hands with him saying that the organization could not get along without him. He was so happy again. His happiness resulted from seeing God in the other fellow and in radiating love and good will to all. True happiness came to him as he began to practice the Presence of God.

Love frees; it gives; it is the spirit of God. Love is the Universal Solvent; for Love dissolves everything unlike Itself.

HARMONIOUS HUMAN RELATIONS

"All things whatsover ye would that men should do unto you, do ye even so to them."

The first thing you learn is that there is no one to change but yourself. The above truth has outer and inner meanings: As you would that men should think about you, think you about them in like manner. As you would that men should feel about you, feel you also about them in like manner. As you would want men to act toward you, act you toward them in like manner. This Biblical passage is the key to happy, human relationships in all walks of life.

Do you observe your "inner talking"? For example, you may be polite and courteous to someone in your office, but when his back is turned, you are very critical and resentful toward him in your mind. Such negative thoughts are highly destructive to you; it is like taking poison; you are actually taking a mental poison which robs you of vitality, enthusiasm,

strength, guidance, and good will.

The suggestion you give to the other, you give to yourself. Ask yourself now, "How am I behaving internally toward this other fellow?" This interior attitude is what counts. Begin now to observe yourself; observe your reactions to people, conditions, and circumstances. How do you respond to the events and news of the day? It makes no difference if all the other people were wrong, and you alone were right, if the news disturbs you, it is your evil, because your bad mood affected and robbed you of peace and harmony. You do not have to react negatively to the news or the comments of the broadcaster. You can remain unmoved, undisturbed, and poised, realizing he has a right to his expression and beliefs. It is never what a person says or does that affects us; it is our reaction to what is said or done that matters.

Mentally divide yourself into two people: Your present mental state and that which you desire to be. Look at the thoughts of envy, jealousy, and hatred which may have enslaved and imprisoned you. You have divided yourself into two people for the purpose of disciplining yourself: One is the race mind working in you, the other is the Infinite or the God-Self seeking expression through you. Be honest with yourself and determine which mood shall prevail.

For example, if someone gossips about you or

criticizes you, what is your reaction? Are you going to engage in the typical way by getting excited, resentful, and angry? If you do, you are letting the world-mind work in you. You must positively refuse to react in this mechanical, stereotyped, machine-like way. Say positively and definitely to yourself: The Infinite One thinks, speaks, and acts through me now; this is my Real Self. I now radiate love, peace, and good will to this person who criticized me. I salute the Divinity in him. God speaks through me as peace, harmony, and love. It is wonderful. You are now a real student of truth. Instead of reacting like the herd who returns hate for hate, you have returned love for hatred, peace for hurt, good will for ill will. You have come into truth to think and react in a new way. When you come into truth, you make a new set of reactions to supplant the old. If you find yourself always reacting in the same way to people and conditions, you are not growing. Instead you are standing still, deeply immersed in the race mind.

You know that you do not have to accept negative thoughts. You can become what you want to be by refusing to be a slave to old, thought patterns.

Become the real observer, and practice observing your reactions to the events of the day. Whenever you discover that you are about to react negatively, say firmly, "This is not the Infinite One speaking or acting"; this will cause you to stop your negative

thinking; then the Divine Love, Light, and Truth will flow through you at that moment. Instead of identifying yourself with anger, resentment, bitterness, and hatefulness, identify immediately with peace, harmony, poise, and balance; with this attitude you are really practicing the art of separation. You are separating yourself from the old (your present, mental state), and you are identifying yourself with the new (that which you desire to be).

You want to be the Christed one, the Anointed individual, the Illumined one, the God-man—who does not? In order to become the ideal, you must identify yourself with all the qualities and attributes you wish to manifest.

Remember this great truth: You do not have to go along with, believe in, nor consent to negative thoughts or reactions. Begin to positively refuse to react mechanically as you formerly did. React and think in a new way. You want to be peaceful, happy, radiant, healthy, prosperous, and inspired; therefore, from this moment forward you must refuse to identify with negative thoughts which tend to drag you down.

Many women say, "How can I change my husband?" Another frequent statement is, "I would like to change Mary in the office; she is the cause of all the trouble." Many have heard the metaphysical phrase, "See the Christ in the other, and all is well." However

most people do not know exactly what that means. It really means to become aware of the Presence of God in the other, and to realize that God is actually being expressed through the thoughts, words, and actions of that person. To really know, accept, and believe these truths is to see the Christ in the other.

There is no problem in human relations that you cannot solve harmoniously and for the benefit of all concerned. When you say that your associate in the office is very difficult to handle, that he is cantankerous, mean, and obstreperous, do you realize that in all probability he is reflecting your own inner mental states. Like attracts like; birds of a feather flock together. Is it not possible that your associate's crotchety, petulant, critical attitude is a reflection of your inner frustrations and suppressed rage? What this person says or does cannot really hurt you, except you permit him to injure you. The only way he can annoy you is through your own thoughts.

For example, if you get angry, you had to go through four stages in your mind: You began to think about what he said; you decided to get angry and generate a mood of rage; then you decided to act—perhaps you talked back and reacted in kind. You see that the thought, emotion, reaction, and action all took place in your mind.

You are the cause of your own anger. If someone

called you a fool, why should you get angry? You know you are not a fool. The other person is undoubtedly very disturbed mentally; maybe his child died during the night, or perhaps he is very ill psychologically. You should have compassion on him, but not condemn him. Realize God's peace fills his mind, and that His Love flows through him; then you would be practicing the Golden Rule. You would be identifying not with anger or hatred but with the law of goodness, truth, and beauty.

Would you condemn a person who had tuberculosis? No, you would not. In all probability if he told you, you would realize the Presence of God, harmony, and perfection where the trouble was; that would be compassion. Compassion is the Wisdom of God functioning through the mind of man, shown when you forgive all men, and see the God in them.

A person who is hateful, spiteful, envious, and jealous, and who says nasty, mean, scandalous things is very ill psychologically; he is just as sick as the man who has tuberculosis. How are you going to react to such a man? Where is your truth? Where is your wisdom and understanding? Are you going to say, "I am one of the herd; I react in kind; I return spite for spite, hate for hate, and anger for anger?" No, you would stop, and say, "This is not the Infinite One acting through me. God sees only perfection, beauty, and harmony. I see, therefore, as God sees." "Thou art

of purer eyes than to behold evil, and canst not look on iniquity." I am going to see all men and women as God sees them. When your eyes are identified with beauty, you will not behold the distorted picture.

Information or news is constantly brought to your attention all day long through the medium of your five senses. You are the one who determines what your mental responses are going to be to the news conveyed. You can remain poised, serene, and calm, or you can fly into a rage, and as a result get an attack of migraine or some other form of pain.

The reason two men react differently to the same situation is based on their subconscious conditioning. Your personality is based on the sum total of all your opinions, beliefs, education, and early religious indoctrination; this inner attitude of mind conditions your response.

One man will fly into a rage when he hears a certain religious program, but his brother may enjoy it, because one is prejudiced and the other is not. Our subconscious convictions and conditioning dictate and control our conscious actions. You can recondition your mind by identifying yourself with the eternal verities. Begin now by filling your mind with the concepts of peace, joy, love, good humor, happiness, and good will. Busy your mind with these ideas; as you do, they will sink into the subconscious

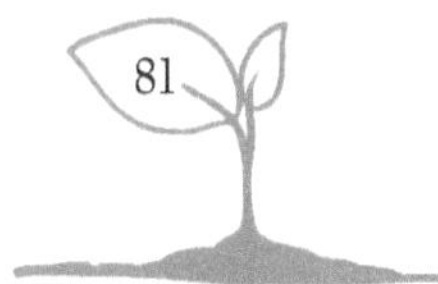

level and become orchids in the garden of God.

No matter where the problem is, how acute it may be, or how difficult the person may be, there is in the final analysis no one to change but yourself! When you change yourself, your world and environment will change. Begin with number one—*yourself!*

You are not living with people, you are living with your concept about them. How are you now responding to John Jones who is next to you on the bench? The fellow who works next to him likes him; his wife loves him; his children think he is wonderful. Perhaps members of his club believe he is generous, kind, and cooperative. Are you thinking of him as mean and petty? Are you resenting him? Who is this fellow? Is he *your* concept, or are all the others wrong? Would it not be wise to look within yourself and determine what it is in you that is causing him to be ugly or a stumbling block to you? I am sure you will find it within yourself.

Maybe you are saying to your son or father when you go home, "That fellow Jones annoys the life out of me. He irritates me beyond words." You are so upset, you cannot digest your dinner properly. According to your description he is impossible.

Where was Jones during the time you were saying all these things? Perhaps he was at the opera with his family; perchance he was out fishing in the stream

having a wonderful, glorious time. As a matter of fact if someone said to you, "Where is Jones now?" You would answer, "I do not know." Be honest with yourself now, and admit he is in your own mind as a thought, a concept, or a mental image. You are revealing yourself and your own perturbed state of mind.

Surely he is not responsible for your anger, tension, or upset stomach. You know in your heart, which is the place that matters, that you are responsible for your own thoughts about him; it is your negative, hostile, reaction to him that is the cause of your trouble. You are the cause of your negative state. Ask yourself, "Who is thinking these things, and who is feeling them? You are!

Quimby used to say that the suggestion we give to the other, we give to ourselves. You can now see how true that is. As a matter of fact, that is the basis of the Golden Rule. Never suggest to another, or think anything about another, that you would not wish the other to think, suggest, or feel about you.

Watch your hidden conversation to yourself. How do you meet people in your mind when they are thousands of miles away? You may be nice to their face, but the way you think about them is what counts. If you are negative, you are poisoning yourself. Does it make any sense to go to a corner drug store, and say,

"I do not like that fellow Jones; give me some poison. I want to take small doses of it several times a day." You are answering now, "Oh, that is absurd!" But that is what you do when you resent or are antagonistic towards others; you are actually taking mental poison which saps your vitality, destroys your enthusiasm, and brings about a debility of the entire organism.

There are mental, corrosive poisons, just the same as there are physical, corrosive poisons; they are just as destructive also. If you are now disturbed, agitated, and angry over the way someone has acted toward you, it means you have a very negative thought-pattern in your consciousness which you should heal instantly.

Be sure that you are not one of those people who will give all the reasons why they should be angry. Stop giving alibis; cease all self-justification. How could you be justified in hating or resenting someone? Do you have a special license? If you do, who gave you this authority? If you are agitated toward another, you are responsible for your unhappiness.

You should not defile the temple of the Living God. Your mind should be a house of prayer; do not make it a den of thieves. The thieves who rob you of peace, joy, health, and happiness are: envy, jealousy, hatred, resentment, and anger. Refuse to harbor these gangsters and assassins.

You do not have to go down the dark alleys and corridors of your mind to consort with thieves and ruffians. Go down the beautifully lit streets of your mind. Jesus or the Truth is always walking down the streets of your mind saying, "Come to God, and find peace, rest, joy, long life, and happiness." As you identify with these truths of God, you have found your saviour. What you identify with, you become. You are transfigured into the image of what you contemplate and feel as true.

When you go to the factory tomorrow, and you meet that fellow or girl whom you say irritates you beyond words, quiet the mind, and say, "He is God's son, and God's Love flows through him. I see the Christ or the Presence of God in him. I see him through the eyes of God, and he is perfect, loving, peaceful, and cooperative." Repeat it quietly to yourself a few times, and go on about your business. Do not bother looking for results. You know results follow your changed mental attitude.

If the old, vicious thought of resentment or anger comes to you during the day, say to yourself quietly, lovingly, and positively, "What is true of God is true of him. I see him as God sees him; it is wonderful to behold God in action in myself, and in him also." You are now observing yourself, because you are refusing to yield to the evil thought; you are identifying with

God or the Good only. A complete healing will follow as you persist in your new way of thinking and reacting. You are, as the Bible tells you, transformed by the renewal of your mind. You have changed your mental and emotional reaction towards others; as a result you have dominion over yourself.

Now you can decree how your thoughts and emotions shall be directed. You are now a king over your own household (mind). Your thoughts, ideas, and feelings are your servants. You issue the command; their mission is to obey. You are here to control, and not to be controlled by angry, wild emotions.

Now when you say to yourself, "Who is the thinker in me?" you must answer, "I am!"

When you are thinking on whatsoever things are true, honest, just, lovely, and of good report, you are truly thinking. If you find yourself thinking negatively, it is the world- mind thinking in you; then you have lost control.

The next time you are prone to resent someone, or when you say that you cannot get along with another, say to yourself, "When I look into his face, I am looking into the face of God; he is an incarnation of God walking this earth. I see God in him, and all is well."

"That thou seest man,

That, too, become thou must;
God, if thou seest God;
Dust if thou seest dust."

HOW TO CONTROL YOUR EMOTIONS

The Ancient Greeks said, "Man, know thyself." As you study yourself, you seem to be made up of four parts: Your physical body, emotional nature, intellect, and the Spiritual Essence which is called the Presence of God. The I AM within you, the Divine Presence, is your Real Identity Which is Eternal.

You are here to discipline yourself, so that your intellectual, emotional, and physical nature are completely spiritualized. These four phases of your nature are called the four beasts of *The Book of Revelation.* {*The Revelation of St. John* means God revealing himself as man.

The real way for you to discipline and bridle your intellectual and emotional nature is by the Practice of the Presence of God all day long.

You have a body; it is a shadow or reflection of the mind. It has no power of itself, no initiative, or volition. It has no intelligence of itself; it is completely subject

to your commands or decrees. Look upon your body as a great disc upon which you play your emotions and beliefs. Being a disc, it will faithfully record all your emotionalized concepts and never deviate from them; therefore, you can register a melody of love and beauty, or one of grief and sorrow upon it. Resentment, jealousy, hatred, anger, and melancholia are all expressed in the body as various diseases. As you learn to control your mental and emotional nature, you will become a channel for the Divine, and release the imprisoned splendor that is within you.

Think over this for a moment: You cannot buy a healthy body with all the money in the world, but you can have health through riches of the mind, such as thoughts of peace, harmony, and perfect health.

Let us dwell now on the emotional nature of man. It is absolutely essential for you to control your emotions if you want to grow spiritually. You are considered grown up or emotionally mature when you control your feelings. If you cannot discipline or bridle your emotions, you are a child even though you are fifty years old.

You must remember that the greatest tyrant is a false idea which controls a man's mind holding him in bondage. The idea you hold about yourself or others induces definite emotions in you. Psychologically speaking, emotions compel you for good or evil. If you

are full of resentment toward someone or possessed by a grudge, this emotion will have an evil influence over you, and govern your actions in a manner which has nothing to do with what you say is the original cause. When you want to be friendly and cordial, you will be ugly, cynical, and sour. When you want to be healthy, successful, and prosperous in life, you will find everything going wrong. Those of you reading this book are aware of your capacity to choose a concept of peace and good will. Accept the idea of peace in your mind, and let it govern, control, and guide you.

Quimby pointed out that ideas are our masters, and that we are slaves to the ideas we entertain. The concept of peace with which you now live will induce the feeling of peace and harmony. Your feeling is the Spirit of God operating at the human level; this feeling of peace and good will will compel you to right action. You are now governed by Divine Ideas which are mothered by the Holy Spirit.

Uncontrolled or undisciplined emotion is destructive. For example, if you have a powerful automobile, it will take you through the roughest country, or to the top of a high hill; however, you must control the automobile. If you do not know how to drive, you may hit a telegraph pole or another car. Should you step on the gas instead of the brake, the car may be destroyed.

It is wonderful to posses a strong, emotional nature provided you are the master. Your emotions are controlling you if you permit yourself to get angry over trifles or agitated over practically nothing. If you get upset over what you read in the newspapers, you are not controlling your emotions. You must learn to blend your intellect and emotions together harmoniously. The intellect of man is alright in its place, but it should be anointed or illumined with the Wisdom of God.

There are many people who are always trying to intellectualize God. You cannot define the Infinite. Spinoza said that to define God is to deny him. You have met the highly intellectual man who says that man cannot survive death, because he does not take his brain with him. Somehow he is so clever he really believes the brain thinks by itself. Such a man is looking at everything from a three-dimensional standpoint; that is where the intellect ceases.

The intellect, as I said previously, is alright in its place—for example, in our everyday work, and in all kinds of science, art, and industry. However as we approach the Living Spirit Almighty within, we are compelled to leave the world of the intellect and go beyond into the realm of spiritual values which are perfection, and where dimension is infinity.

When man's intellect is blended with the

emotions of love, peace, and goodwill, he will not use explosives and knowledge of chemistry for the destruction of mankind. The reason man uses the atomic bomb, submarine, and other implements of warfare to destroy his fellow creature is because his spiritual awareness and knowledge lag so far behind his intellectual achievements.

Let us see how emotions are generated. Suppose you observe a cripple; perhaps you are moved to pity. On the other hand you may look at your young, beautiful child, and you feel an emotion of love welling up within you. You know that you cannot imagine an emotion, but if you imagine an unpleasant episode or event of the past, you induce the corresponding emotion. Remember it is essential to entertain the thought first before you induce an emotion.

An emotion is always the working out of an idea in the mind. Have you noticed the effect of fear upon the face, eyes, heart, and other organs? You know the effect of bad news or grief on the digestive tract. Observe the change that takes place when it is found the fear is groundless.

All negative emotions are destructive and depress the vital forces of the body. A chronic worrier usually has trouble with digestion. If something very pleasant occurs in his experience, the digestion becomes normal, because normal circulation is restored,

and the necessary gastric secretions are no longer interfered with.

The way to overcome and discipline the emotions is not through repression or suppression. When you repress an emotion, the energy accumulates in the subconscious and remains snarled there. In the same manner as the pressure increases in the boiler, if all the valves are closed, and you increase the heat of the fire, finally there will be an explosion.

Today in the field of psychosomatic we are discovering that many cases of ill health, as arthritis, asthma, cardiac troubles, and failure in life, etc., may be due to suppressed or repressed emotions, perhaps occurring during early life or childhood.

These repressed or suppressed emotions rise like ghosts to haunt you later on. There is a spiritual and psychological way to banish these ghosts which walk in the gloomy gallery of your mind. The ideal way is the law of substitution. Through the law of mental substitution, you substitute a positive, constructive thought for the negative. When negative thoughts enter your mind, do not fight them; just think of God and His Love; you will find the negative thoughts disappear. "I say unto you, That ye resist not evil." (Math. 5:39) If a person is fearful, the positive emotion of faith and confidence will completely destroy it.

If you sincerely wish to govern your emotions, you must maintain control over your thoughts. By taking charge of your thoughts, you can substitute love for fear. The instant you receive the stimulus of a negative emotion supplant it with the mood of love and good will. Instead of giving way to fear, say, "One with God is a majority." Fill your mind with concepts of peace, love, and faith in God; then the negative thoughts cannot enter.

It is far easier to cremate, burn up, and destroy negative thoughts at the moment they enter the mind, rather than try and dislodge them when they have taken possession of your mind. Refuse to be a victim of negative emotions through controlling your thought and thinking of God and His Attributes. You can be master of all emotions and conditions. "He that is slow to anger is better than the mighty; and he that ruleth his spirit than he that taketh a city."

The Book of Revelation deals with the control of the intellectual and emotional life of man. It says in Chapter 4, verses 6, 7, and 8: "And before the throne *there was* a sea of glass like unto crystal: and in the midst of the throne, and round about the throne, were four beasts full of eyes before and behind.

"And the first beasts was like a lion, and the second beasts like a calf, and the third beast had a face as a man, and the fourth beast was like a flying eagle.

"And the four beasts had each of them six wings about *him*; and *they were* full of eyes within: and they rest not day and night, saying, Holy, holy, holy, Lord God Almighty, which was, and is, and is to come."

The sea of glass before the throne means the inner peace of God, for God is peace. Deep in the centre of your being, the Infinite One lies stretched in smiling repose. It is the Living Presence of God within you. You stand before this throne. *The throne* is a symbol of authority. Your emotional conviction of a deep, abiding faith in the God- Power is your authority in consciousness. To say it simply: Your inner conviction is your throne in heaven, because therein lies your power. "According to your faith is it done unto you." *Faith* is a positive, emotional attitude knowing that the good I seek is mine now.

The four beasts forever before the throne are the four phases of your being: spiritual, mental, emotional, and physical. In order to get your emotional nature on a spiritual basis, it is necessary to understand these four beasts; in doing so you learn the gentle art of scientific prayer which in the final analysis is the answer to all problems. Study these four potencies of consciousness.

The lion is the king of the jungle; it means God, your I AMNESS.

Taurus means the bull or beast of burden. Your

burden is your desire. You labor in your imagination to make your desire a part of your consciousness.

Aquarius means the water bearer; it means meditation. The word *meditation* means to eat of God or your good, to feast upon your ideal. You pour water on your ideal, meaning you dwell upon and pour love on it which is the water of life. Something happens as you mentally feast upon your ideal; you generate an emotion; the latter is the spirit of God moving on your behalf. Your emotion is the Holy Spirit moving at human levels. God is a reactive, reciprocal Power within you. Your emotion responds according to the nature of the idea. As you emotionalize your idea, it sinks into the subconscious mind as an impression; this is called the *Eagle* or *Scorpio*, meaning the Divine impregnation. These are the four stages of the unfoldment or manifestation of an ideal or desire. Whatever is impressed is expressed.

The four beasts had each of them six wings. *The six wings* refer to the mental, creative act. When idea and feeling blend together in harmony and faith, there has taken place a wedding ceremony in the mind. Knowledge of this mental, creative act gives you wings; enables you to soar aloft above the storms and struggles of the world, and find peace and strength in your own mind.

Let us take an illustration explaining the story of

spiritual and mental creation: In the name *Jehovah* is concealed the perfect way to pray scientifically; thereby bringing all discordant emotions under scientific control. Jehovah, Yod-He-Vau-He, is composed of four letters. *Yod* means God, or I AM; *He* means desire or idea; *Vau* is feeling or conviction; the final *He* is the manifestation of what you felt as true inside. The third letter *Vau* is considered the most important of all. It enables you to feel you are that which you desire to be. Walk in the mental atmosphere that you now are what you want to be; this mood will jell within you, and you will experience the joy of the answered prayer. The word *Vau* also means nail. *To nail* your desire is to fix it in consciousness, so that you are at peace about it.

Remember you do not have to live in a world of sickness and confusion created by your own errors or ignorance. You have the power and the capacity to imagine and feel you are what you desire to be. As you completely accept your desire mentally, that you now are what you wish to be, through mental absorption, you have completed the name or the creative way of God as portrayed in the name: *Yod-He-Vau-He.* In other words you have completed the creative process in your own mind as outlined by Troward in his *Bible Mystery and Bible Meaning.* To know how to pray scientifically is to be able to control your emotions. "More things are wrought by prayer than this world dreams of."

CASE HISTORIES

Case History Number One

Let us take some cases histories. A soldier who has returned from Korea told me that when he was seized with fear, he would say to himself over and over again, "God's Love surrounds me, and goes before me." This affirmation impressed his mind with the feeling of love and faith. This mood of love supplanted his fear. "Perfect Love casteth out fear." This procedure is the answer to the process of freedom from fear.

Case History Number Two

A mother, whose only child died, was grief stricken. The grief was affecting her vision, and she suffered from migraine headaches. She was in a deep state of depression. I suggested to her that she go to a hospital and offer her services in the children's ward. She was a former nurse. In offering her time at a local hospital, she began to pour out love on the children; she coddled them; cared for them, and fed them. The love was no longer bottled up within her; she became a channel for the Divine, and began to release the sunshine of God's Love. She practiced sublimation which was a redirection of the energy lodged within her subconscious mind. In this manner she drained off the poison pockets of her subconscious mind.

Case History Number Three

A woman who comes to our meeting told me that she was accustomed to fits of temper and anger periodically by the action of neighbors. Instead of letting the anger and hatred affect her mentally and physically by pushing it back into the subconscious, she transmuted it into muscular energy by getting a gallon of water and washing the windows or the floor. Sometimes she would begin to dig in the garden, saying to herself aloud, "I am digging in the garden of God, and planting God's ideas." She would do this for fifteen minutes at a time. When washing the windows, she would say aloud, "I am cleansing my mind with the waters of love and life." The above illustrations are simple methods of working off negative emotions in a physical way.

CHANGING
THE FEELING OF "I"

"If you say "I," to everything you think, feel, say, or imagine, you cannot transform your emotional life. Remember all kinds of thoughts can enter your mind; all kinds of emotions may enter your heart. If you say, "I," to all negative thoughts, you are identifying yourself with them, and you cannot separate internally from them. You can refuse to attach "I" to negative emotions and thoughts.

You make it a practice to avoid muddy places as you walk along the road; likewise you must avoid walking down the muddy roads of your mind where fear, resentment, hostility, and ill-will lurk and move. Refuse to listen to negative remarks. Do not touch the negative moods, or let them touch you. Practice inner separation by getting a new feeling about yourself, and about what you really are. Begin to realize that the real "I" in you is the Infinite Spirit, the Infinite One. Begin to identify yourself with the Qualities and

Attributes of this Infinite One; then your whole life will be transformed.

The whole secret in transforming your negative, emotional nature is to practice self-observation. To observe, and *to observe* oneself are two different things. When you say, "You observe . . ." you mean you give your attention to external things. In self-observation the attention is directed inwards.

A man may spend his whole life-time studying the atom, stars, body, and the phenomenalistic world—namely, knowledge of the external world; this knowledge cannot bring about an interior change. Self-observations is the means of interior change — the change of the heart.

You must learn to differentiate, to discern, to separate the chaff from the wheat. You practice the art of self-observation when you begin to ask yourself, "Is this idea true? Will it bless, heal, and inspire me? Will it give me peace of mind, and contribute to the well-being of humanity?"

You are living in two worlds: the external and the internal; yet they are both one. One is visible and the other invisible (subjective and objective). Your external world enters through your five senses, and is shared by everyone. Your internal world of thought, feelings, sensations, beliefs, and reaction is invisible and belongs to you.

Ask yourself, "In which world do I live? Do I live in the world revealed by my five senses, or in this inner world?" It is in this inner world you live all the time; this is where you feel and suffer.

Suppose you are invited to a banquet. All you see, hear, taste, smell, and touch belong to the external world. All that you think, feel, like, and dislike belong to the inner world. You attend two banquets recorded differently: namely, one the outer, and one the inner. It is in your inner world of thought, feeling, and emotion in which you rise and fall and sway to and fro.

In order to transform yourself, you must begin to change the inner world through the purification of the emotions, and the correct ordering of the mind through right thinking. If you want to grow spiritually, you must transform yourself.

Transformation means the changing of one thing into another. There are many well-known transformations of matter. Sugar through a process of distillation is changed into alcohol; radium slowly changes into lead, etc. The food you eat is transformed, stage by stage into all substances necessary for your existence.

Your experiences coming in as impressions must be similarly transformed. Suppose you see a person you love and admire; you receive impressions about him. Suppose on the other hand you meet a person

you dislike; you receive impressions also.

Your husband or daughter sitting on the couch as you read this is to you what you conceive him or her to be. In other words impressions are received by your mind. If you were deaf, you would not hear their voices. You can change your impressions of people. To transform your impression is to transform yourself. To change your life, change your reactions to life. Do you find yourself reacting in stereotyped ways? If your reactions are negative, that is your life. Never permit your life to be a series of negative reactions to the impressions that come to you everyday.

In order truly to observe yourself, you must see that regardless of what happens, your thought and feeling are fixed on this great truth: "How is it in God and Heaven?" This will lift you up and transform all your negative thoughts and emotions. You may be inclined to say that other people are to blame, because of the way they talk or act, but if what they say or do makes you negative, you are inwardly disturbed; this negative state is where you now live, move, and have your being.

You cannot afford to be negative; it depletes your vitality; robs you of enthusiasm, and makes you physically and mentally ill. Do you live in the room where you are now? or do you live in your thoughts, feelings, emotions, hopes, and despair? Is it not

what you are feeling about your environment now, that is real to you? When you say, "My name is John Jones," what do you mean? Is it not a fact that you are a product of your thinking, plus the customs, traditions, and the influence of those around you as you grew up? You are really the sum-total of your beliefs, opinions, plus what you have derived from your education, environmental conditioning, and the countless other influences acting upon you from the external world and entering through your external senses.

Perhaps you are now comparing yourself with others. Do you feel inferior in the presence of a person who seems to be more distinguished than you are? Suppose you are a great pianist—when someone praises another pianist, do you feel inferior? If you have the real feeling of "I," this would not be possible; for the true feeling of "I" is the feeling of the Presence of the Infinite One in you, in Which there are no comparisons.

Ouspensky used to point out that people became upset easily, because their feeling of "I" was derived from negative states of consciousness. The feeling of "I" was one of his favorite expressions, and some of his ideas are incorporated in this chapter.

I said to a man in our Bible class recently, "Have you observed your typical reactions to people,

newspaper articles, and radio commentators? Have you noticed your usual, stereotyped behaviour?"

He replied, "No, I have not noticed these things." He was taking himself for granted, and not growing spiritually. He began to think about his reactions; then he admitted that many of the articles and the commentators irritated him immensely. He reacted in a machine-like manner and was not disciplining himself. It makes no difference if all the writers and commentators were wrong, and he, alone, was right; the negative emotion aroused in him is destructive; it shows lack of mental and spiritual discipline.

When you say, "I think this . . ." "I think that . . ." "I resent this . . ." or "I dislike this . . ." which "I" is speaking? Is it not a different "I" speaking every moment? Each "I" is completely different. One "I" in you criticizes one moment; a few minutes later another "I" speaks tenderly. Look at and learn about your different "I's," and know deep within yourself that certain "I's" will never dominate, control, or direct your thinking.

Take a good look at the "I's" you are consorting with. With what kind of people do you associate? I am referring to the people that inhabit your mind. Remember your mind is a city; thoughts, ideas, opinions, feelings, sensations, and beliefs dwell

there. Some of the places in your mind are slums and dangerous streets; however Jesus (your saviour) is always walking down the streets of your mind in the form of your ideal, desire, and aim in life.

One of the meanings of Jesus is your desire; for your desire, when realized, is your saviour. Your aims and objectives in life are now beckoning to you; move toward them. Give your desire your attention; in other words take a lively interest in it. Go down the streets of love, peace, joy, and good will in your mind; you will meet wonderful people on the way. You will find beautifully, lighted streets and wonderful citizens on the better streets of your mind.

Never permit your house, which is your mind, to be full of servants which you do not have under control. When you were young, you were taught not to go with what your mother called, "bad company." Now when you begin to awaken to your inner powers, you must make it a special point that you do not go with wrong "IV (thoughts) within you.

I had an interesting chat with a young man who studied mental discipline in France. His procedure was to take, as he said, "mental photographs of himself from time to time." He would sit down, and think about his emotions, moods, thoughts, sensations, reactions, and his tones of voice; then he would say, "These are not of God; they are false. I will go back to

God and think from that Standard or Rock of Truth." He practiced the art of inner separation. He would stop when he got angry, and say, "This is not the Infinite One, the real 'I' speaking, thinking, or acting; it is the false 'I' in me."

Return to God like this young man. Every time you are prone to get angry, critical, depressed, or irritable, think of God and Heaven, and ask yourself, "How is it in God and Heaven?" *There* is the answer to becoming the new man; this is how you become spiritually reborn or experience what is called the second birth. {*The second birth is* internal discipline and spiritual understanding.)

The saint and the sinner are in all of us; so are the murderer and the holy man; likewise are God and the world mind. Every man basically and fundamentally wants to be good, to express good, and to do good. This is "the positive" in you. If you have committed destructive acts, as for example, if you have robbed, cheated, and defrauded others, and they condemn you, and they hold you in a bad light, you can rise out of the slum of your mind to that place in your own consciousness where you cease to condemn yourself; then all your accusers must still their tongues. When you cease to accuse yourself, the world will no longer accuse you; this is the power of your own consciousness; It is the God in you.

It is foolish to condemn yourself; you do not have to. It is idle to keep company with the thoughts of self-accusation. Suppose you committed acts of injustice, criminal acts, or other dastardly crimes. It was not the God in you that did those things; it was not the real "I" or the Infinite One, it was the other self (the world-mind) in you. This will not, of course, excuse you from your responsibility, no more so than if you put your hand in the fire, you get burned; or if you pass a red light, you will get a ticket for traffic violation.

The other self represents the many "I" in you, for instance the many negative ideas and beliefs that there are powers outside your own consciousness; the belief that others can hurt you; the elements are unfriendly, plus the fears, superstitions, and ignorance of all kinds. Finally prejudices, fears, and hates drive and goad you to do that which you would not otherwise do. The ideal way to change the feeling of "I" is to affix to the real "I" within you everything that is noble, wonderful, and God-like.

Begin to affirm, "I am strong. I am radiant. I am happy. I am inspired. I am illumined. I am loving. I am kind. I am harmonious." Feel these states of mind; affirm them, and believe them; then you will begin to truly live in the Garden of God. Whatever you affix to the "I AM" and believe, you become. The "I AM" in you is God, and there is none other. "I AM" or Life,

Awareness, Pure Being, Existence, or the Real Self of you is God. It is the Only Cause. It is the Only Power making anything in the world. Honor It; live with the feeling, "I AM Christ," all day long. Christ means the Anointed One, the Awakened One, the Illumined One. Feel you are this Anointed One; continue to live in that mental atmosphere; then you will draw out the Christ (Wisdom, Power, and Intelligence of God) within you, and your whole world will be transformed by that Inner Light shining in your mind. Every-time you feel, "I AM the Christ"; "I AM illumined"; "I AM inspired"; you are praying and qualifying your consciousness with the thing you are praying about, and with the thoughts you are thinking.

As you continue to change the feeling of "I" as outlined above, you will populate the heavens of your mind with God's Eternal Verities: "Fear not for I am with thee; and through the rivers, they shall not overflow thee: when thou walkest through the fire, thou shall not be burned." Who is That One? It is your own I AMNESS; It is the Light or Awareness within you which always goes before you whithersoever thou goest. Your dominant mental attitude or atmosphere is going ahead of you all the time, creating the experiences you will encounter.

Keep in mind that when you pray about any specific thing, it is necessary to qualify your mind with the consciousness or *feeling of having or being that*

109

thing. You mentally reject completely the arguments in your mind against it; that is prayer. Qualify your consciousness with the thing you are praying for by thinking about it with interest. Do this quietly and regularly until a conviction is reached in your consciousness. As you do this, the problem will no longer annoy you. You will maintain your mental poise, plus the feeling of: "I now feel that I am what I long to be," and as you continue to feel it, you will become it.

Here is the law: "I am that which I feel myself to be." Practice changing the feeling of "I" every day by affirming: "I am Spirit; I think, see, feel, and live as Spirit, the Presence of God. (The other self in you thinks, feels, and acts as the race mind does.) As you continue to do this, you will begin to feel you are one with God. As the sun in the heavens redeems the earth from darkness and gloom, so will the realization of the Presence of God in you reveal the man you always wished to be—the joyous, radiant, peaceful, prosperous, and successful man whose intellect is illumined by the Light from above.

God causes the sun to shine on all men everywhere. No man can take away the sunshine of God's Love from you. No one can place you in the prison of fear or ignorance when you know the Truth of God which sets you free.

The feeling that the "I AM" in you is God reveals to you that there is nothing to be afraid of, and that you are one with Omnipotence, Omniscience, and Omnipresence. No one can steal health, peace, joy, or happiness from you. You no longer live with the many "IV of fear, doubt, and superstition. You now live in the Divine Presence, and in the consciousness of freedom.

Ask yourself, "Who is it that takes charge of me at every moment, and speaks in His Name, calling Itself "I"? Never identify with this other man (fear, prejudice, pride, arrogance, condemnation, etc.). You now realize you need not go in the direction of negative "Ps." You will never again say, "Yes," to any idle, negative thought; neither will you give it the sanction and signature of yourself.

Become the observer by keeping your eyes fixed on God—the real "I"—the Infinite One within you. Feel the sense of "I" on the observing side, and not in what you are observing. Feel that you are looking out through the eyes of God; therefore, "*Thou art* of purer eyes than to behold evil, and canst not look on iniquity."

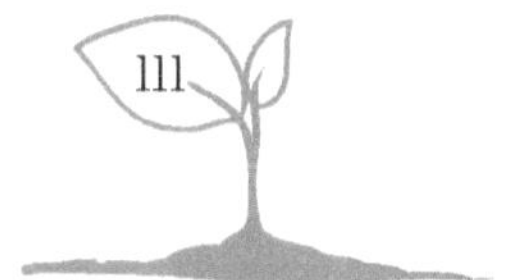

LIST OF TITLES WITH ISBN NO.

ISBN	TITLE
9788194914129	1984
9789390575220	1984 & Animal Farm (2In1)
9789390575572	1984 & Animal Farm (2In1): The International Best-Selling Classics
9789390575848	35 Sonnets
9789390575329	A Clergyman's Daughter
9789390575923	A Study In Scarlet
9789390896097	A Tale Of Two Cities
9789390896837	Abide in Christ
9789390896202	Abraham Lincoln
9789390896912	Absolute Surrender
9789390896608	African American Classic Collection
9789390575305	Aldous Huxley: The Collected Works
9789390896141	An Autobiography of M. K. Gandhi
9789390575886	Animal Farm
9789390575619	Animal Farm & The Great Gatsby (2In1)
9789390575626	Animal Farm & We
9789390896158	Anna Karenina
9789390575534	Antic Hay
9789390896165	Antony & Cleopatra
9789390896172	As I Lay Dying
9789390896226	As You like it
9789390575671	At Your Command
9789390575350	Awakened Imagination
9789390575114	Be What You Wish
9789390896233	Believe In yourself
9789390896998	Best of Charles Darwin: The Origin of Species & Autobiography
9789390896684	Best Of Horror : Dracula And Frankenstein
9789390575503	Best Of Mark Twain (The Adventures of Tom Sawyer AND The Adventures of Huckleberry Finn)
9789390896769	Black History Collection
9789390575756	Brave New World, Animal Farm & 1984 (3in1)

9789390896240	Brother Karamzov
9789390575053	Bulleh Shah Poetry
9789390575725	Burmese Days
9789390896257	Bushido
9789390896066	Can't Hurt Me
9788194914112	Chanakya Neeti: With The Complete Sutras
9789390896042	Crime and Punishment
9789390575527	Crome Yellow
9789390575046	Down and Out in Paris and London
9789390896844	Dracula
9789390575442	Emersons Essays: The Complete First & Second Series (Self-Reliance & Other Essays)
9789390575749	Emma
9789390575817	Essential Tozer Collection - The Pursuit of God & The Purpose of Man
9789390896578	Fascism What It Is and How to Fight It
9789390575688	Feeling is the Secret
9789390575190	Five Lessons
9789390575954	Frankenstein
9789390575237	Franz Kafka: Collected Works
9789390575282	Franz Kafka: Short Stories
9789390575060	George Orwell Collected Works
9789390575077	George Orwell Essays
9789390575213	George Orwell Poems
9788194914150	Greatest Poetry Ever Written Vol 1
9788194914143	Greatest Poetry Ever Written Vol 1
9789390896301	Gulliver's Travel
9789390575961	Gunaho Ka Devta
9789390575893	H. P. Lovecraft Selected Stories Vol 1
9789390575978	H. P. Lovecraft Selected Stories Vol 2
9789390896059	Hamlet
9789390575022	His Last Bow: Some Reminiscences of Sherlock Holmes
9789390896134	History of Western Philosophy
9789390575121	Homage To Catalonia

9789390896219	How to develop self-confidence and Improve public Speaking
9789390896295	How to enjoy your life and your Job
9789390575633	How to own your own mind
9789390896318	How to read Human Nature
9789390896325	How to sell your way through the life
9789390896370	How to use the laws of mind
9789390896387	How to use the power of prayer
9789390896028	How to win friends & Influence People
9788194824176	How To Win Friends and Influence People
9789390896103	Humility The Beauty of Holiness
9789390896653	Imperialism the Highest Stage of Capitalism
9789390575084	In Our Time
9789390575169	In Our Time & Three Stories and Ten poems
9789390575145	James Allen: The Collected Works
9789390896189	Jesus Himself
9789390575480	Jo's Boys
9789390896394	Julius Caesar
9789390575404	Keep the Aspidistra Flying
9789390896400	Kidnapped
9789390896424	King Lear
9789390575824	Lady Susan
9789390896455	Law of Success
9789390896264	Lincoln The Unknown
9789390575565	Little Men
9789390575640	Little Women
9788194914174	Lost Horizon
9789390896462	Macbeth
9789390896929	Man Eaters of Kumaon
9789390896523	Man The Dwelling Place of God
9789390896349	Man The Dwelling Place of God
9789390575909	Mansfield Park
9788194914136	Manto Ki 25 Sarvshreshth Kahaniya
9789390896509	Marxism, Anarchism, Communism
9789390575664	Mathematical Principles of Natural Philosophy

9788194914198	Meditations
9789390575800	Mein Kampf
9789390575794	Memory How To Develop, Train, And Use It
9789390896486	Mind Power
9789390896585	Money
9789390575039	Mortal Coils
9789390575770	My Life and Work
9789390896035	Narrative of the Life of Frederick Douglass
9789390575152	Neville Goddard: The Collected Works
9789390575985	Northanger Abbey
9789390896530	Notes From Underground
9789390896547	Oliver Twist
9789390575459	On War
9789390575541	One, None and a Hundred Thousand
9789390896554	Othelo
9789390575435	Out Of This World
9789390575015	Persuasion
9789390575510	Prayer The Art Of Believing
9789390575091	Pride and Prejudice
9789390896561	Psychic Perception
9789390575381	Rabindranath Tagore - 5 Best Short Stories Vol 2
9789390575367	Rabindranath Tagore - Short Stories (Masters Collections Including The Childs Return)
9789390575374	Rabindranath Tagore 5 Best Short Stories Vol 1 (Including The Childs Return
9789390896622	Romeo & Juliet
9789390896127	Sanatana Dharma
9789390575596	Seedtime & Harvest
9789390896639	Selected Stories of Guy De Maupassant
9789390575206	Self-Reliance & Other Essays
9789390575176	Sense and Sensibility
9789390575299	Shyamchi Aai
9789390896738	Socialism Utopian and Scientific
9789390896646	Success Through a Positive Mental Attitude
9789390575428	The Adventures of Huckleberry Finn

9789390575183	The Adventures of Sherlock Holmes
9789390575343	The Adventures of Tom Sawyer
9789390896691	The Alchemy Of Happiness
9789390575862	The Art Of Public Speaking
9789390896288	The Autobiography Of Charles Darwin
9788194914181	The Best of Franz Kafka: The Metamorphosis & The Trial
9789390575008	The Call Of Cthulhu and Other Weird Tales
9789390575107	The Case-Book of Sherlock Holmes
9789390896110	The Castle Of Otranto
9789390896745	The Communist Manifesto
9789390575589	The Complete Fiction of H. P. Lovecraft
9789390575497	The Complete Works of Florence Scovel Shinn
9789390896820	The Conquest of Breard
9789390896813	The Diary of a Young Girl
9789390896332	The Diary of a Young Girl The Definitive Edition of the Worlds Most Famous Diary
9789390575701	The Great Gatsby, Animal Farm & 1984 (3In1)
9789390575312	The Greatest Works Of George Orwell (5 Books) Including 1984 & Non-Fiction
9789390575992	The Hound of Baskervilles
9789390896707	The Idiot
9789390896714	The Invisible Man
9789390575657	The Knowledge of the holy
9789390575558	The Law & the Promise
9789390896721	The Law Of Attraction
9789390896776	The Leader in you
9789390896363	The Life of Christ
9789390896196	The Man-Eating Leopard of Rudraprayag
9789390896783	The Master Key to Riches
9789390575268	The Memoirs Of Sherlock Holmes
9789390896479	The Midsummer Night's Dream
9789390575466	The Mill On The Floss
9789390896790	The Miracles of your mind
9789390896660	The Mutual Aid A Factor in Evolution
9789390896448	The Origin of Species

9789390896905	The Peter Kropotkin Anthology The Conquest of Bread & Mutual Aid A Factor of Evolution
9789390896806	The Picture of Dorian Gray
9789390896271	The Picture of Dorian Gray
9789390575275	The Power Of Awareness
9789390896356	The Power of Concentration
9788194824169	The Power of Positive Thinking
9789390575411	The Power of the Spoken Word
9788194914105	The Power Of Your Subconscious Mind
9789390896899	The Power of Your Subconscious Mind
9789390896417	The Principles of Communism
9789390575787	The Psychology Of Mans Possible Evolution
9789390896615	The Psychology of Salesmanship
9789390575732	The Pursuit of God
9789390575398	The Pursuit of Happiness
9789390896851	The Quick and Easy Way to effective Speaking
9789390575947	The Return Of Sherlock Holmes
9789390575138	The Road To Wigan Pier
9789390896981	The Root of the Righteous
9789390575855	The Science Of Being Well
9788194914167	The Science Of Getting Rich, The Science Of Being Great & The Science Of Being Well (3In1)
9789390896011	The Screwtape Letters
9789390896073	The Screwtape Letters
9789390575336	The Secret Door to Success
9789390575695	The Secret Of Imagining
9789390896868	The Secret Of Success
9789390896431	The Seven Last Words
9789390575930	The Sign of the Four
9789390896004	The Sonnets
9789390896516	The Souls of Black Folk
9789390896875	The Sound and The Fury
9789390575244	The State and Revolution
9789390896882	The Story of My Life
9789390896936	The Story Of Oriental Philosophy

9789390896752	The Strange Case of Dr. Jekyll and Mr. Hyde
9789390896943	The Tempest
9789390575916	The Valley Of Fear
9789390575879	The Wind in the willows
9789390896080	The Wind in the willows
9789390575763	Their eyes were watching gofd
9789390575831	Three Stories
9789390896950	Twelfth Night
9789390896592	Twelve Years a Slave
9789390896677	Up from Slavery
9789390896974	Value Price and Profit
9789390896967	Wake Up and Live
9789390896493	With Christ in the School of Prayer
9789390575602	Your Faith is Your Fortune
9789390575473	Your Infinite Power To Be Rich
9789390575251	Your Word is Your Wand
9789390575718	Youth
9789391316099	A Christmas Carol
9789391316105	A Doll's House
9789391316501	A Passage to India
9789391316709	A Portrait of the Artist as a Young Man
9789391316112	A Tale of Two Cities
9789391316747	A Tear and a Smile
9789391316167	Agnes Gray
9789391316174	Alice's Adventures in Wonderland
9789391316136	Anandamath
9789391316181	Anne Of Green Gables
9789391316754	Anthem
9789391316198	Around The World in 80 Days
9789391316013	As A Man Thinketh
9789391316242	Autobiography of a Yogi
9789391316266	Beyond Good and Evil
9789391316761	Bleak House
9789391316778	Chitra, a Play in One Act
9789391316310	David Copperfield

9789391316075	Demian
9789391316785	Dubliners
9789391316051	Favourite Tales from the Arabian Nights
9789391316235	Gitanjali
9789391316068	Gravity
9789391316150	Great Speeches of Abraham Lincoln
9789391316662	Guerilla Warfare
9789391316839	Kim
9789391316822	Mother
9789391316211	My Childhood
9789391316846	Nationalism
9789391316327	Oliver Twist
9789391316853	Pygmalion
9789391316334	Relativity: The Special and the General Theory
9789391316389	Scientific Healing Affirmation
9789391316341	Sons and Lovers
9789391316587	Tales from India
9789391316372	Tess of The D'Urbervilles
9789391316396	The Awakening and Selected Stories
9789391316402	The Bhagvad Gita
9789391316303	The Book of Enoch
9789391316228	The Canterville Ghost
9789391316907	The Dynamic Laws of Prosperity
9789391316006	The Great Gatsby
9789391316860	The Hungry Stones and Other Stories
9789391316433	The Idiot
9789391316440	The Importance of Being Earnest
9789391316297	The Light of Asia
9789391316914	The Madman His Parables and Poems
9789391316457	The Odyssey
9789391316921	The Picture of Dorian Gray
9789391316464	The Prince
9789391316938	The Prophet
9789391316945	The Republic
9789391316518	The Scarlet Letter

9789391316143	The Seven Laws of Teaching
9789391316525	The Story of My Experiments with Truth
9789391316532	The Tales of the Mother Goose
9789391316549	The Thirty Nine Steps
9789391316594	The Time Machine
9789391316600	The Turn of the Screw
9789391316983	The Upanishads
9789391316617	The Yellow Wallpaper
9789391316426	The Yoga Sutras of Patanjali
9789391316990	Ulysses
9789391316624	Utopia
9789391316679	Vanity Fair
9789391316020	What Is To Be Done
9789391316686	Within A Budding Grove
9789391316693	Women in Love